At Issue

| Open Borders

Other Books in the At Issue Series

At Issue

| Open Borders

Andrew Karpan, Book Editor

GREENHAVEN
PUBLISHING

Published in 2021 by Greenhaven Publishing, LLC
353 3rd Avenue, Suite 255, New York, NY 10010

Articles in Greenhaven Publishing anthologies are often edited for length to meet page
requirements. In addition, original titles of these works are changed to clearly present
the main thesis and to explicitly indicate the author's opinion. Every effort is made to
ensure that Greenhaven Publishing accurately reflects the original intent of the authors.
Every effort has been made to trace the owners of the copyrighted material.

Cover image: gualtiero boffi/Shutterstock.com

Library of Congress Cataloging-in-Publication Data

Names: Karpan, Andrew, editor.
Title: Open borders / Andrew Karpan, book editor.
Other titles: Open borders (Greenhaven Publishing)
Description: New York : Greenhaven Publishing, 2021. | Series: At issue |
  Includes bibliographical references and index. | Audience: Grades 9-12.
Identifiers: LCCN 2019060163 | ISBN 9781534507395 (library binding) | ISBN
  9781534507388 (paperback)
Subjects: LCSH: Emigration and immigration--Social aspects--Juvenile
  literature. | Emigration and immigration--Economic aspects--Juvenile
  literature. | Emigration and immigration--Government policy--Juvenile
  literature. | Freedom of movement--Juvenile literature.
Classification: LCC JV6225 .O638 2021 | DDC 304.8--dc23
LC record available at https://lccn.loc.gov/2019060163

Manufactured in the United States of America

Website: http://greenhavenpublishing.com

Contents

Introduction

The Trump administration's policy of cracking down on illegal immigration at the Mexican-American border (beginning in 2016) may well be one of the last gasps of nationalism in American politics. The superseding force of global economics has made border patrol feel like a vestige of the past when applied to goods and services, and the idea that the free movement of people may soon follow in its wake has come to seem less like a utopian dream and more like an inevitibility.

In simple terms, open borders are those that allow people to move freely between countries with limited restriction and border control. The current concept of open borders was a creation of the post-war era. It was signified by the creation of institutions like the United Nations—which was created in 1945 following the Second World War partially to hash out agreements promising that borders around the world would be open to refugees—and the World Trade Organization, which was created in 1995 following the end of the Cold War and committed itself to opening those same borders to trade. On the relatively local level, agreements like the Schengen Agreement in 1985 and the North American Free Trade agreement in 1994 created common zones of trade and travel among some of the world's biggest economies. These moments were revolutionary. In Western Europe, the Schengen Agreement removed impediments to travel between countries that had been engulfed in territorial military conflict less than half a century earlier. In North America, the free trade agreement created a shared economic zone that remains one of the largest in the world.

More recent immigration politics have shown the strain of adjusting what remains of century-old political systems and cultural institutions to the new globalized economy and culture rushing to replace them. The US-Mexican border had been born out of violence, created by the Treaty of Hidalgo (1848) that ended the Mexican-American War (1846-1848), but its more recent life as a conduit of refugee movement from Central America into the United States dominated border politics in the early Trump Administration. "I have absolute power to shut down the border," he told the *New York Times* in 2019,[1] a statement that masks the difficulty of shutting down the 2,000 miles of interconnected highways and cities that mark this border. While this proclamation did not result in decreased trade or even fewer people crossing the border, it brought to public attention a humanitarian crisis: children and their families were detained in overcrowded US border stations in the summers of 2018 and 2019, "wearing clothes caked with snot and tears."[2] With the conditions of these detainment centers brought to light, debate over the ethics and practicalities of border patrol was reinvigorated.

Political events in other parts of the world followed the same logic, including the 2016 Brexit referendum in the UK, the ongoing conflict between India and Pakistan over the Kashmir region, and the anti-European Union sentiments animating the yellow vest movement in Paris. However, the material conditions of borders stayed the same regardless of their role in the political imagination. Refugees from the Syrian Civil War, which lasted through much of the 2010s, would stay in camps in and around cities of Western Europe, but little else would change. When one country closes its borders to refugees, these displaced individuals must simply find somewhere else to go. What these events indicated was that despite the particularities of the circumstances, they are all part of a larger global trend, and consequently must be solved on an international scale. Even a movement like the 2018 yellow vests protests in Paris, which ostensibly targeted a new tax leveled by the Macron administration, would not occur without, as Jon Henley noted in the *Guardian*, multiplying "internationally, from Belgium to Bulgaria, Serbia to Sweden and Israel to Iraq."[3]

In many cases, the concerns are fundamentally economic. A world with open borders is a world that would, on some level, have to share the same labor laws and handle shared costs. Large companies were the first to take advantage of those new conditions in the form of multinational corporations, and their global workforces were the first to feel that change. With industry moving to other countries through the process of globalization, the economy of the United States—once among the world's centers of industrial production—suddenly became a service economy endlessly providing for the wealth it had concentrated. In this sense, while a more globalized economy tends to clearly benefit corporations, the effect it has on countries tends to be more complicated.

Another complication is that a world with free movement can also create populations left without countries to call home. The UN's High Commissioner for Refugees estimates that "nearly 25.9 million" people as of mid-2019 had been forced to flee their countries of origin.[4] These refugees leave behind their countries for a number of reasons, ranging from war, to religious or political persecution, to climate disasters. As a result, they wade between borders indefinitely through a trans-national network of refugee settlements.

Elsewhere, an even larger number of people make these journeys temporarily as tourists. Per the UN's World Tourism Organization, some 1.4 billion people —more than the population of any single country—traveled internationally in 2018.[5] Once a luxurious privilege of the statistically insignificant wealthy class, the tourist is now a ubiquitous presence, and borders are constantly relaxing to accommodate their transit. Tourism offers economic opportunities and the potential for greater understanding between people from around the world, but the question of who should have the privilege of crossing borders with limited scrutiny while others are restricted from freely moving between countries is a source of controversy.

The viewpoints in *At Issue: Open Borders* illustrate what the current border zones of the twenty-first century look like. They tackle the dream of an open-bordered world and the reality of crossing borders today from a range of economic, political, and social perspectives to promote greater understanding of this complicated issue.

Notes

[1] Michael D. Shear and Julie Hirschfeld Davis, "Shoot Migrants' Legs, Build Alligator Moat: Behind Trump's Ideas for Border," *New York Times*, October 1, 2019.

[2] Caitlin Dickerson, "'There Is a Stench': Soiled Clothes and No Baths for Migrant Children at a Texas Center." *New York Times,* June 21, 2019.

[3] Jon Henley, "How hi-vis yellow vest became symbol of protest beyond France, the *Guardian*, December 21, 2015.

[4] "Figures at a Glance," United Nations High Commissioner for Refugees, 2019.

[5] "International Tourism Highlights: 2019 Edition," United Nations World Tourism Organization, 2019.

1

Cross-Border Trouble

Julie Grant

Julie Grant is a longtime reporter and producer for North Country Public Radio, an NPR affiliate run by St. Lawrence University in New York's North Country, which abuts the Canadian border.

The US-Canadian border is the longest contiguous border between any two nations in the world and, for the most part, it has been one of the friendliest. It is a largely unguarded expanse of five thousand miles that has facilitated trade between two of the most powerful nations in the Western world. Since the September 11 terrorist attacks, Julie Grant writes, that border has become a spot of tension: a weak spot ready to be abused by malicious terrorists. Thousands of border agents now guard those miles by ground, air, and boat. Fishermen in the Great Lakes are among those inconvenienced by the changes in policy.

In the years since the September 11 attacks, life has changed along the U.S. – Canadian border. What used to be an informal crossing, has become militarized, and its changed the lives and expectations of people who live nearby. Julie Grant takes a look back at some of ways life has changed along the border, and whether it's making Americans safer.

People in towns along the border used to cross back and forth between Canada and the U.S. all the time for everything from

"U.S.-Canadian border changes since 9/11," by Julie Grant, North Country Public Radio, September 9, 2011. Reprinted by permission.

dinner and shopping to cheaper gas. Customs might have waved you through without even checking for I-D. People bragged about how friendly it all was.

But then, September 11 happened. In the days after, newspapers mistakenly reported that some of the attackers had entered the U.S. through Canada. The mistake stuck. Eight years later, U.S. Secretary of Homeland Security Janet Napolitano repeated it. She later backtracked, then told Fox News:

> But the point is this, and this is the greater point, there's been some resistance or feeling in Canada that we are thickening the border unnecessarily between our two countries, and the answer is that Canada allows people in its country that the United States does not necessarily allow in the United States.

The U.S. has spent billions of dollars beefing up its northern border since September 11: Upgrading ports of entry, increasing surveillance and technology, more than doubling the number of border officers. Now, everyone coming in from Canada needs a passport, or another official form of identification.

Nowadays, homeland security can stop drivers even when they're not crossing the border. David Sommerstein reported in 2005 about the increasing presence of border patrols along north country roadways:

> This is a border patrol checkpoint on Route 37 between Masenna and Ogdensburg. The agent may wave you through quickly, or you may have to answer several questions. The U.S. border patrol is allowed to set up roadblocks within 100 air miles of the border. The agency says it has 20-30 locations around northern New York and Vermont. On Interstate 91, Interstate 87 in Essex County, and on local roads, mostly in Jefferson, St. Lawrence, and Franklin Counties.

Homeland security officers have also started checking passports on buses travelling in New York, and other states—anything within 100 miles of the border is fair game.

The stops have become more intrusive in recent years.

Last year, American student Pascal Abidor was trying to cross the border while travelling home to New York City by Amtrak train. He was detained at the crossing north of Plattsburgh.

"They asked everything about my life. My interests, why I'm interested in Islam, why I've travelled in the Middle East. Eventually when I received the lap top back, I looked at the last open date of files, and based on that I was able to determine that they had looked extensively at my personal photos, personal saved chats with my girlfriend."

The American Civil Liberties Union and two other groups have filed suit against the Department of Homeland Security, based in part on Abidor's incident. The case is still in the courts.

Civil liberties advocates say stories like Abidor's show the types of freedoms Americans have given up since September 11.

The thicker northern border has also made it hard to do business across the border.

For example, Boldt Castle in the Thousand Islands says new U.S. security requirements have dramatically reduced the number of tourist boats that can come over from Canada; numbers of boats are down from nine a day to two and that's a loss of about 420-thousand dollars a year.

Bob Runciman of Brockville represents the Thousand Islands in Canada's Senate. He says it's essential to businesses on both sides that border crossings go smoothly.

"If you have to sit in a line at a bridge for over an hour to come over for dinner or go to the theatre or do some shopping, you're not going to do that very often."

Politicians on both sides of the border have searched for a balance for the last ten years. They want the border open for business, while maintaining security, but it's proven tough.

"It's tougher than ever for the businessman" said Mark Barie of Plattsburgh. He calls himself Captain of the Canadian Connection. Barie worked for 30 years helping Canadian businessmen get work visas, but he sold the business two years ago because, now more than ever, immigration authorities are hitting businesses hard.

"Either they bang them in without any questions at all, or they drive them crazy until they give up. You need an experienced immigration practitioner to get through the border these days. It shouldn't be that way."

But the top priority at the border isn't free trade, it's security.

U.S. security secretary Janet Napolitano has said that when suspected or known terrorists have entered the U.S. across a border, it's been across the Canadian border.

Which begs the question: For all the time, money, and goodwill spent, is the U.S. safer?

Chris Kirkey, director of the Center for the study of Canada at SUNY Plattsburgh, answers, "Yes, absolutely."

"With the increase in the number of agents, the increase in and the sophistication in the training they receive, and the regularity of that training, as well as the new technology that's in place and will continue to be put in place. The ability, while not perfect, the ability to potentially detect and avert any kind of threat to the United States is at the highest level that it's ever been. There's no question about that."

But in 2007, the General Accountability Office (GAO) released a report showing that the Canadian border posed a significant threat as a terrorist point of entry. Brian Mann spoke with the managing director of investigations at the GAO, Greg Kutz.

Kutz said his team was able to cross the border easily at four remote sites along the Canadian border.

Kutz said, "At several of these locations we simulated smuggling radioactive materials and other contraband into the U.S. At one location, our investigator delivered a large red duffel bag about 75 feet from a rental car parked in Canada, to a rental car parked in the U.S."

For obvious reasons, Brian said Kutz wouldn't disclose which sites were used for the crossing, but he did say at least one of the crossings on the northern border involved an actual checkpoint that had been closed for the night.

"The other vulnerability we identified on the northern border related to ports of entry with posted daytime hours that were unmanned over night," Kutz said.

According to Brian, the GAO was able to drive a car around a traffic barrier erected at the checkpoint.

More recently, in February this year, a GAO report found that only 32 miles of the 4-thousand mile U.S.-Canada border is secure. The Department of Homeland Security says they are confident about security along a thousand miles.

In 2007, Brian also spoke with Congressman John McHugh (now secretary of the army) about the problem of patrolling such a long border:

"I guess one of the concerns would be that this border is so vast, and so porous currently, that we'll get to the place where we're hassling the heck out of people who are trying to come across for legitimate reasons, but someone who's a wanted felon in Canada can choose an empty stretch of dirt road and walk across," said Brian.

"Well, or walk across one of the many islands in the St. Lawrence." McHugh responded, "We could hire ten million new border agents and have them stand along the border hand to hand and we still wouldn't have an absolutely tight border."

Despite the daunting logistics, however, security has continued to increase.

This summer, boaters and fishermen were shocked by the latest escalation in border enforcement.

When an American drifted into Canadian waters while fishing on the St. Lawrence River, Canadian agents boarded his boat and fined him.

The agents said he needed to check in at a port of entry even though he hadn't anchored or docked. American boaters didn't know they needed to check in with Canada when drifting because, for generations, they just didn't.

Fishermen from both shores have been drifting on the St. Lawrence since before there was a border. But others say no one should be surprised that tougher border enforcements have reached so far into daily life. The days of informality on the border between Canada and the United States are ten years in the past.

2

The State of the African Union

Kerry Dimmer

Kerry Dimmer is a freelance writer based in South Africa whose writing has appeared in African Decisions Leadership, Mining Decisions, *and* Breakbulk Magazine, *as well as* Africa Renewal, *a publication run by the Africa Section of the United Nations Department of Global Communications.*

No continent in the world has more countries than Africa, which, since the end of colonial rule, split into fifty-four separate nations. Institutions such as the African Union—which was formed in 2002 to take the place of the Organisation of African Unity (originally formed in 1963)—are vital to the continent's cross-border economic and political stability. As Kerry Dimmer writes, these organizations could form the basis for a visa union, which could bring those fifty-plus nations closer together than ever before.

Would an Africa in which Africans require no visas to travel boost prospects for intracontinental trade?

The African Union (AU) and many of the continent's economic organisations think so and want it to be a reality by 2020. It is not an entirely original concept (the European Union already has a visa-free policy for its citizens), and many experts laud the AU's position, at least in principle.

"A visa-free Africa still facing hurdles," by Kerry Dimmer, Africa Renewal, United Nations, December 2017-March 2018. Reprinted by permission.

The idea of an African passport dates back a quarter of a century but has failed to catch on with countries that fear an increase in smuggling, illegal immigration, terrorism, and the spread of disease as well as a negative impact on local job markets. With migration, legal and illegal, blamed for recent outbreaks of xenophobia in South Africa, some of these fears seem credible.

Visa-free travel for Africans in Africa could be a logistical nightmare given that some citizens do not have travel documents and others lead nomadic lives. Individual countries may need to enact legislation to adopt the African passport. Few African nations use the biometric data that an African passport requires.

African Passport

Last year the AU launched an African passport, a signature project of former chairperson Nkosazana Dlamini-Zuma. However, the passport is currently available only to senior diplomats and top officials of AU's 55 member states.

Of those member states, only Seychelles offers visa-free access to all African countries. "The large and fast-growing economies aren't following suit because the visa regime itself has created a bureaucratic habit," notes Daniel Silke, director of the South Africa–based Political Futures Consultancy.

"Old habits are hard to break, although there is justification for hesitation in terms of the legitimate layer of security that visas provide."

Mr. Silke adds that growing and large economies worry about the impact that increased population movements might have on labour markets and cities. Some of Africa's fast-growing economies are Côte d'Ivoire, Ethiopia, Guinea, Senegal and Tanzania. Out of desperation, thousands of immigrants travel to South Africa, the continent's largest economy, to find work.

"With urban cities expanding rapidly across Africa, government institutions are strained, and cities that offer opportunities for trade, health care, a booming labour market, infrastructure, among others, will be under increased pressure," notes Mr. Silke.

He suggests a focus on efficient and affordable visa procurement processes, advising regional communities to enact and implement policies that make it easier for their citizens to move from one member state to another.

In November 2017, after 15 years of negotiations, the Central African Economic and Monetary Community (CEMAC), comprising of Cameroon, Central African Republic, Chad, Equatorial Guinea, Gabon and the Republic of Congo, ratified the visa-free movement of its citizens.

Under the policy, member states will adopt biometric technology, ensure police and security services' coordination, and respect for different labour regulations.

The next best thing to a visa-free system is visa on arrival, which may include authorization to stay for up to 90 days. Rwanda adopted this protocol in 2013 and has witnessed an increase in African visitors and investors, noted Mr. Anaclet Kalibata, the country's director general of immigration and emigration.

Mr. Kalibata told Africa Renewal that between 2013 and 2016, the number of Africans receiving visas on arrival at Rwandan entry points increased by more than 100%. "We have also hosted many more conferences as a result of the removal of travel restrictions," he said.

"Most of the people entering our country do so for good reasons," said Mr. Kalibata. He pointed out that Rwanda has "laws governing criminality associated with the movement of people. We also believe in competitiveness in terms of skills…. So, opening our borders has attracted new talent and investment."

Like Rwanda, Ghana now offers visa-free access to a third of AU member states and visas on arrival to the other two-thirds. In so doing, the country has made the most progress of all African states toward a visa-free Africa for Africans, according to the Africa Visa Openness Report 2017 by the African Development Bank (AfDB).

Senegal is offering visa-free access to 42 African countries in a bid to reenergize its tourism sector.

At his swearing in as Kenya's president last November, Uhuru Kenyatta announced that all Africans will henceforth receive visa on arrival.

An alternative to adopting visa-free access or visas on arrival is for countries to enter into reciprocal arrangements with other nations. Namibian authorities are making efforts to finalise such arrangements, meaning that citizens of countries allowing Namibians visas on arrival will receive reciprocal service at Namibian ports of entry.

Although Rwanda already offers Africans visa on arrival, it is also receptive to reciprocal arrangements with other countries, explained Mr. Kalibata. "We've proven just how effective unrestricted regional travel can be through the issue of a unified national identity card and border pass for citizens of Uganda, Kenya and Rwanda.

"Another border pass agreement between Rwanda, the DRC, Burundi, Tanzania and Uganda has fostered regional social cohesion, and we've seen cross-border trade in our countries now contributing 42% to GDP, which is very significant," he added.

Rwanda's experience, however, is not enough to change the perception of the negative impacts of liberalizing entry visas. Jean-Guy Afrika, AfDB's principal policy expert and a contributor to the Africa Visa Openness Report 2017, notes, "The 2016 analysis of Africa's visa policy regimes demonstrated that on average Africans needed visas at departure to travel to 54% of other African countries (from 55% in 2015); could get visas on arrival in only 24% (from 25% in 2015); and do not need visas to travel to just 22% (from 20% in 2015)."

The reasons African countries remain closed to each other, says Mr. Afrika, vary significantly. "The key reasons advanced by policy makers generally relate to fears of job losses and security concerns. But there could also be issues of culture and trust. The answer probably lies somewhere in the nexus between politics, culture, history and economics."

Visa Liberalization

Mr. Afrika confirms that at the regional level, East and West Africa lead in visa openness. "In the 2017 rankings of the Africa Visa Openness Index, 75% of countries in the top 20 are in these two regions. Only one is in the North and none in Central Africa."

The AfDB, the AU and the World Economic Forum Global Agenda Council on Africa collaborated on the Africa Visa Openness Report 2017, the second of its kind. Researchers gathered data from the International Air Transport Association and from responses to questionnaires administered to national focal points.

"Overall the trend is positive, given that just four years ago only five countries offered liberal, arrival or no visa, access to citizens of all African countries. Today that number stands at 14, but we want that number to keep moving up," Mr. Afrika says.

Visa liberalization is not a magic bullet, he cautions, even if it can foster Africa's integration. He recommends other reforms and massive investments in connectivity to complement visa liberalization, citing Rwanda as an example of a country benefiting from coordinated investments and policy reforms, including in business and air transport infrastructure.

"Visa openness may only be one piece of the interconnected African states puzzle, but it is nonetheless a very important one," concludes Mr. Afrika.

3

Open Borders Would Benefit Africa, but Careful Planning Is Necessary

Terence Corrigan

Terence Corrigan is a former SAIIA researcher in the program on African Governance and Diplomacy.

In order to allow for economic growth and greater unity across the continent, since 2015 the African Union has aimed to remove visa requirements for Africans traveling across the continent, with the ultimate goal of a common African passport. While some nations have made strides in opening their borders, most countries still require visas for entry, and for many of these countries visas must be obtained prior to travel. Until all borders are open to visa-free access, it will not be possible to implement an African Union passport for citizens of all African countries.

Whether described as "African Unity" or "integration," and whether for ideological or pragmatic reasons, overcoming the fragmentation of the continent has been an enduring theme in African statecraft since the 1960s. The borders dividing Africa's 55 states from one another, so this reasoning goes, have lessened Africa's global presence and kept markets small and anaemic. They have also prevented its citizens from reaching out to one another

"Africa with open borders: A possibility or a pipe dream?" by Terence Corrigan, africaportal.org, a project of the South African Institute of International Affairs (SAIIA) and the Centre for International Governance Innovation (CIGI), December 7, 2017. Reprinted by permission.

and taking advantage of the vast potential that the continent has to offer.

Adopted in 2015, the African Union's (AU's) long-term development blueprint, Agenda 2063, pledged to bring about free movement of African citizens across the continent. It envisioned that all visa requirements for travel by Africans within the continent would be abolished by 2018, and a common African passport introduced by 2025.

How is this progressing?

According to the 2017 Visa Openness Report—an initiative of the African Development Bank, the African Union Commission and the World Economic Forum Global Agenda Council on Africa—progress on creating a 'visa-free Africa' has been modest. The report looks at the accessibility of Africa's 55 countries to visitors from each of the others.

It analyses the requirements that each African country imposes on visitors from other countries on the continent in terms of a three-phase model: how many countries' citizens are required to obtain visas prior to travel; how many countries' citizens are able to obtain visas on arrival; and how many countries' citizens can enter the country with no visa at all.

In 2016 (the period covered by the report), there were 2,970 requirements imposed by African countries on other African citizens—in other words, each of the 55 countries had a visa or non-visa requirement for each of the other 54 countries. Of these, a little over half (54%) were for visas to be obtained prior to departure. This suggests that, on balance, Africa's borders remain closed. Just over a fifth or requirements (22%) were for no visas, and around a quarter (24%) were for visas on arrival.

Only one country, the Seychelles, was truly "visa free"—it granted citizens of every other African country entry with no visa, and had no requirement that they obtain one upon entry.

The greatest strides in openness have been made among island states, and East and West Africa. Rwanda and Ghana stand out as countries that have made particular progress.

Ghana introduced a new visa regime in 2016, extending visa-free or visa-on-arrival access to the citizens of all AU countries. Rwanda has been opening up its borders to African travellers since 2013—accommodating all AU visitors with visas on arrival—and recently announced that this would be extended to all countries at the beginning of 2018.

Most recently, Kenya has followed suit in opening its borders. In late November 2017, newly inaugurated President Uhuru Kenyatta announced that citizens of all African countries would be able to obtain a visa on arrival.

But open borders are a far from the norm in Africa. Most countries retain visa requirements vis-à-vis the citizens of other African countries. The northern, central and southern parts of Africa, as well as its wealthier countries have taken less ambitious action on openness.

Jeggan Grey-Johnson of the Open Society Foundation's Africa regional office questions the manner in which the AU has conceptualised an open-border regime. He argues that the idea of opening up Africa's borders speaks to a long-standing aspiration, but it is not ideally suited to an AU or pan-African rollout. Rather, borders should open to facilitate practical exchanges among the continent's people—the starting point should be reciprocal freedom of movement between neighbours. In this context, the key obstacle to free movement of people has been the failure of Africa's Regional Economic Communities (RECs)—the Economic Community of West African States excepted—to take it seriously.

In addition, Grey-Johnson points to the lack of leadership on freedom of movement provided by regional hegemons, such as South Africa and Angola in the Southern African Development Community. Perhaps because they are likely to attract migrants—with the possibility that this will fuel economic and socio-political stresses—such countries have been lukewarm in their support for free movement. "Africa's powerhouses," Grey-Johnson remarks, "are holding integration back."

AU Passport

Opening up Africa's borders by way of visa free access is seen (officially) by the AU as a prelude to the introduction of an AU passport. Launched at an AU summit in Kigali in July 2016, the document is in very limited circulation. It is currently available to AU staff, national leaders and select officials from AU member states. The first were presented to Chad's President Idriss Déby, and to the summit host, Rwanda's President Paul Kagame. It has been reported that prominent Nigerian entrepreneur Aliko Dangote is to be issued with one.

In theory, a continental passport should make visas redundant and imply open borders for all. The official narrative is that it is to be made available to ordinary citizens by the middle of the next decade. There is, however, little clarity about how this will be implemented.

Veteran South African journalist Peter Fabricius remarks that there was some unintended symbolism in presenting the first AU passports to heads of state: "This sent a symbolic message that it was for elites, not the ordinary populace. Governments will decide which of their citizens get it and also whether to recognise passport holders from other countries. So, it seems likely that it might go to some influential business people but not much further for a while."

An AU passport would raise a number of issues that go beyond mere freedom of movement and to the heart of the long-term ideals of African integration. Passports do not serve only as travel documents but also as signifiers of citizenship. Would this be the case in respect of an AU passport? If so, what rights and obligations would that confer on its holders? Would it imply not only the right to travel, but the right of settlement? And if it does indeed denote such expanded rights, can it justifiably be withheld from the broader population while being made available to a small group of elites? Conversely, would African countries that are fearful of their ability to handle increased migration be reluctant to recognise an emerging AU citizenship?

Added to this is the thorny issue of stateless people and refugees: those who are clearly of the continent without a stable relationship to any country. Would this compromise their claims to AU citizenship?

Each of these issues will inevitably arise as the AU passport becomes more common. Firm and satisfactory responses will need to be crafted—they do not exist at present.

A continent of free movement, an AU passport and the possibility of pan-African citizenship rights—these are alluring aspirations, but at present, they remain for most of the continent largely in the realm of aspiration. With some exceptions, rhetoric on these issues far exceeds reality. There is very little prospect of a visa-free Africa or a common passport in general use in the foreseeable future. These goals will best be achieved through recommitting to ground-level action aimed at practical outcomes.

For example, opening borders—where possible, through the continent's RECs—should in the first instance seek to facilitate linkages between neighbours so as to encourage trade and tourism. Continental ambitions can come later. The rollout of the African passport, likewise, needs to be meticulously planned if it is indeed to signify a new and inclusive chapter in African integration.

Africa has no shortage of symbolism. Now it requires resolute action.

4

Open Hypocrisy in the British Commonwealth

David Olusoga

David Olusoga teaches public history at the University of Manchester and has presented numerous documentaries for the BBC. He also writes regularly for the Guardian.

Around the same time that continental Europe began the lengthy process of opening its borders, the United Kingdom did the same for its former colonies in 1948, offering them common citizenship in an effort to fill labor shortages within Britain. The Windrush generation followed, an influx of immigrants from Caribbean nations that David Olusoga writes had been unwanted by many British citizens. The borders had been opened to ensure the continued flow of economic trade, but the immigrants themselves suffered a kind of second-class citizenship, which came to widespread attention in the Windrush scandal of 2018.

Late one afternoon last month, in a meeting room in the offices where I work in north London, I sat and wept. This is not something I make a habit of. My own tears were provoked by the tears of Judy Griffiths, a central interviewee in *The Unwanted: The Secret Windrush Files*, a documentary we had then just completed.

Judy had come to our offices to watch sections of the programme, to let us know if she was happy with how we'd portrayed her story. Tough, educated and resilient, she is one of a number of

"Windrush: Archived documents show the long betrayal," by David Olusoga, Guardian News and Media Ltd, June 16, 2019. Reprinted by permission.

victims (or perhaps survivors) of the Windrush scandal that we interviewed for the film.

Even for her, with her level of drive and resourcefulness, taking on a cold, officious and target-driven immigration system was draining and damaging. Yet, in one way, Judy was comparatively fortunate. She happened to have kept hold of some of the documents that the Home Office demanded in order to demonstrate her long residence in the UK. She was also able to track down other scraps of evidence needed to prove something that should never have been in question.

That paper trail, gathered by a woman who has lived and worked in the UK for more than 50 years, included the antenatal records of her now adult children. Others caught in the dragnet of the so-called "hostile environment," and unable to provide similar documents, were dragged into the lower circles of immigration-law hell.

I cried last month not only because Judy cried, but because I was enormously relieved that our film meant something to her. I don't know exactly what brought her to tears. My guess would be that seeing herself and her story framed within a TV documentary brought home, in new ways, the staggering injustice of what she has been through, and reminded her of the obvious—that none of it should ever have happened.

But Judy also cried because the film contains an interview with a friend she had recently made and recently lost—Sarah O'Conner, another victim of the scandal. Sarah had moved to Britain aged six and, after 51 years' residence, had suddenly been refused employment and then benefits. Like Judy she had been forced to become a campaigner for the rights of the so-called Windrush generation. But in September 2018, after a minor operation, she died, aged 57.

The Windrush scandal is raw, shocking and ongoing. The damage done is hard to appreciate until you sit down and listen to the testimony of those affected. When the first of Amelia Gentleman's articles appeared in the *Guardian*, revealing that

British citizens, born in the Caribbean but resident in Britain for many decades, were being denied employment, benefits and healthcare under the hostile environment, a storm of raised voices and hard questions erupted.

David Lammy, visibly angry, gave one of the most impassioned speeches of recent parliamentary history. Even Piers Morgan looked genuinely hot under the collar on breakfast TV when he expressed outrage at the fact that Anthony Bryan—another of the interviewees in *The Unwanted*—was still waiting for his status to be resolved.

It is testimony to the scale and severity of the Windrush scandal that it was able to command enough media bandwidth and enough headspace within the national consciousness to cut through the background Brexit hubbub. For an outrage to metastasize into full-blown, Defcon-1 national scandal in 2018 it needed to be really, really bad.

During the final, farcical attempts to push her Brexit deal through parliament, Theresa May was said to have worried about her political "legacy." Her place in history will only become apparent when the Brexit nightmare is, somehow, resolved. There is no question, however, about how May will be remembered by black Britons. Her legacy within that community is set in stone and has little to do with her three dismal years in Downing Street.

May will be remembered as the home secretary who sent vans with "Go Home" blazoned on their sides to patrol our multicultural cities. The politician who, in 2012, declared her intent "to create, here in Britain, a really hostile environment for illegal immigrants." That soundbite, intended for short-term media consumption, has become May's epitaph and a chapter heading—alongside "colour bar," "rivers of blood" and "sus laws"—in a long and troubled history.

In the 18th century, when the ancestors of the Windrush generation were being shipped in chains to the islands of the Caribbean, the doublethink that was an intrinsic feature of the imperial project was briefly exposed. The challenge came when people who had been enslaved under the laws that then governed Britain's slave colonies were brought to Britain by their "owners." Some absconded and claimed their freedom. It fell to the judges to determine if those defined as human property in the colonies remained so once they set foot in Britain or, if by breathing in British air, they were freed and magically became legal persons. Ultimately they decided slavery was not legal within Britain.

Something similar in terms of exposing a doublethink happened after 1948. Then, black and brown people who had been told their whole lives that they were British subjects with the right to come to the "mother country" began to exercise those rights. In 1948, Britain was asked to cash that promissory note. Instead, the charade was exposed because the principle of free movement within the empire, long a hallowed tenet of the imperial project, had in reality only ever been intended to apply to white people.

Postwar Britain, battered and near bankrupt, was desperate to cling on to as much of the empire as possible—rebranding it the British Commonwealth. Politicians, both Labour and Conservative, were united in their determination that Britain should retain her status as a "world power"—albeit a poor relation to the US and USSR in the age of the superpowers. Key to achieving this, they believed, were the bonds between Britain and the nations of the old Commonwealth—Australia, Canada, New Zealand and South Africa—sometimes tellingly referred to as the "white dominions".

When, in 1948, parliament passed a new British Nationality Act the aim was to reaffirm existing rights that enabled the two-way flow, between Britain and the old Commonwealth, of people who were regularly described in postwar official documents as "our stock," "our people" or people of "British stock." What the politicians failed to predict was that even as they were debating the act, 492 black people from the Caribbean would board the Empire Windrush and exercise their rights as British subjects to work and live in the UK.

The big historical truth that we have yet to confront is wrapped up with the same painful truth that explains how the Windrush scandal of 2018 could have happened—that the arrival of the Empire Windrush in 1948 was unplanned and unexpected. The people on board were unwanted and their moment of arrival set in train two oppositional processes.

It established 1948 as the symbolic beginning of the postwar migration that created modern, multiracial Britain. At the same time it provoked a political struggle that saw successive British governments, both Labour and Conservative, set out to design and introduce laws to limit what they called "coloured migration."

The great dilemma they faced was that any act that put limits on migration of British subjects from all parts of the empire would inevitably limit the movement of white people from the "white dominions". Whereas draft legislation that overtly targeted the black and brown people would damage Britain's standing in the world and undermine the creation of the Commonwealth—the rebranded, reimagined version of the empire that included newly independent states, as well as the old dominions. In an interview in 1954, Winston Churchill's private secretary Sir David Hunt explained the dilemma: "The minute we said we've got to keep these black chaps out, the whole Commonwealth lark would have blown up."

The political struggles of the period that followed the arrival of the Windrush are recorded on the pages of hundreds of documents held at the National Archives. What they reveal is that even before the Windrush set sail from Kingston, British politicians had concluded that "coloured migration" automatically represented a "colour problem" and was thus to be discouraged and curtailed. The other deeper and more fundamental and unquestioned belief that runs through those thousands of archival pages is that black and brown people could never really be British.

The old racism of imperialism not only rendered the postwar political elite unable to see black people as full British citizens, it provided them with a whole glossary of stereotypes and preconceptions that they then deployed in order to justify their aim of introducing immigration controls. In the late 40s and early 50s, a series of studies was launched in Whitehall.

The function of the studies was to find evidence of problems supposedly caused by the presence of black migrants. One study, by the Working Party on Coloured People Seeking Employment in the United Kingdom, reported in late 1953. It concluded, despite much evidence to the contrary, that "coloured workers" struggled to find employment in the UK, and that such difficulties were caused by their "irresponsibility, quarrelsomeness and lack of discipline." The report also stated that black men were "slow mentally" and in general were "not up to the standards required by British employers."

British business came to a different conclusion. Several major employers not only hired Caribbean migrants, but actively recruited them directly from the West Indies. By 1956, London Transport was recruiting in Barbados, even loaning migrants the costs of their passage to Britain. British Rail placed ads in the Barbados Labour Office and the NHS appealed to West Indian women to come to Britain and train to become nurses. It was these companies that issued the invitation to the "mother country" that Britain's postwar governments withheld.

Despite the efforts of five governmental studies there was no evidence that "coloured migration" led to a "colour problem." Even worse, there was sparse evidence that the public was particularly interested. Minutes from meetings of Churchill's cabinet from the mid-50s reveal that politicians were well aware "coloured migration" was not an issue about which there was any deep public concern.

In a meeting in June 1955, the cabinet debated "proposals for the appointment of an independent committee of enquiry into coloured migration," noting that "the first purpose of an enquiry should be to ensure that the public ... were made aware of the nature and extent of the problem: until this was more widely appreciated the need for restrictive legislation would not be recognized." In another meeting, in November 1955, the cabinet concluded that "the problem of colonial immigration has not yet aroused general public anxiety, although there was some concern mainly due to housing difficulties in a few localities where most of the recent immigrants were concentrated."

It was not until 1962, after the public mood *had* grown more hostile, that Harold Macmillan's government finally hit upon a mechanism by which the migration of black and brown people could be limited without curtailing the movement of white citizens of the "old Commonwealth." The 1962 Commonwealth Immigrants Act used a voucher system based upon employment prospects to determine who was able to enter the UK.

A government working party, set up to explore the options, concluded that this was "the only workable method of controlling immigration from the Commonwealth without either bringing such immigration to a virtual standstill or ostensibly discriminating against immigrants on a basis of colour." The key word is "ostensibly."

Another confidential minute noted that while the new system "would apply equally to all parts of the Commonwealth, without distinction on ground of race and colour, in practice it would interfere to the minimum extent with the entry of persons from the 'old' Commonwealth." The then home secretary, Rab Butler, was clear that the act's "restrictive effect is intended to, and would, in fact, operate on coloured people almost exclusively."

The 1962 act was the great watershed, the end of the charade. And there are strands of legislative DNA that stretch from that moment, through the Immigration Act of 1971 and the later immigration laws passed under David Cameron, that removed the legal safeguards that shielded the Windrush generation, all the way to the Windrush scandal of 2018.

The deeper historical roots of the scandal, however, lie not in laws but in beliefs. The belief that Britishness is the same as whiteness, and that black and brown people can never truly be British, no matter what the laws say or what is written on their passports. Such beliefs were held, almost universally, by postwar-era politicians.

In the late 20th century, when the multiracial society they were unable to envisage emerged, such notions should have perished. That they did not goes some way to explaining how the scandal of 2018 happened.

5

Climate Without Borders

Jason Hickel

Jason Hickel is a professor at the University of London who recently wrote a book called The Divide: A Brief Guide to Global Inequality and Its Solution. *He writes for the* Guardian, Foreign Policy, *and* Al Jazeera.

An alternative argument for the opening of borders is the climate crisis, which will likely dominate international politics for much of the next century. Jason Hickel argues that the crisis is impossible to engage with on a nation-by-nation scale. So many of the outright causes of climate change come from countries that have consciously insulated themselves from the consequences. The politics of open borders is both a moral and practical concern.

Europe is facing its biggest refugee crisis since World War II. What is new this time around is that many of the displaced are being driven from their homes by the destructive effects of climate change. And this is just the beginning.

As sea levels rise, swallowing island nations and swamping large parts of Bangladesh, and as droughts trigger food shortages across much of the global South, the refugee crisis will only worsen. And we can expect that Europe's right-wing parties will respond by doubling down on their already-potent anti-immigrant rhetoric with a push to seal off the borders.

"To stop climate change, we need to open borders," by Jason Hickel, Al Jazeera, February 23, 2018. Reprinted by permission.

Pundits on the left denounce this as a craven, mean-spirited stance towards those who are suffering the most from our collective climate crisis. And they're right: opening the borders to climate refugees is a matter of basic justice. We need to devise policies to ensure that all have the right to access safe and habitable parts of the planet we share.

But there is something more to be said here. An open border policy may also be the key to stopping climate change itself.

Scientists tell us that on our present trajectory we have only a 5 percent chance of keeping global warming below the danger threshold of 2 degrees, as our addiction to endlessly expanding economic growth and consumption is swiftly wiping out the gains we're making through technology and renewable energy. As a recent op-ed in the New York Times put it, "The climate crisis? It's capitalism, stupid." We need a new economic system—one that does not require this mad rush up an exponential curve—but our leaders are unwilling to take that step. There is a yawning gap between the threat posed by climate breakdown and how little we are doing to address it.

This is a puzzle. Why are we so willing to gamble thus with the fate of human civilization, with 95 percent certainty of catastrophe? Is it that we're in denial? Are we just repressing a reality that's too traumatic to confront? Yes, probably. But it's also something much simpler: a geography problem.

The great irony of global warming is that its causes and consequences are inversely distributed. The rich nations of the global North are responsible for 70 percent of historical CO_2 emissions, but they bear only about 18 percent of the total costs. It's the South that takes the hit: according to the Climate Vulnerability Monitor, the global South loses nearly $600bn each year due to drought, floods, landslides, storms and wildfires. As climate change worsens, their losses will reach a staggering $1 trillion per year by 2030.

And then there's the human toll. Global warming claims some 400,000 lives each year worldwide—many due to extreme weather events but most due to climate change-induced hunger and disease. Only 2 percent of these deaths occur in the North. The South suffers the rest, and the vast majority of climate mortality occurs in the countries with the lowest carbon emissions in the world.

Yes, Britain has its floods, southern Europe its droughts, and the United States its hurricanes. But as devastating as these are for ordinary people's lives, those governments have so far absorbed the costs and kept chugging along with the status quo—more growth, more consumption, more emissions, more capitalism. They are not acting on climate change because they have no real reason to care. The consequences of their industrial over-consumption are harming lands far beyond their borders.

It's a textbook case of moral hazard: they are willing to take the risk because someone else bears the cost. Of course, eventually, this will change. They will get serious when their coastal cities flood and their food imports dry up—but by then it will be too late.

The solution is simple, at least conceptually: open the borders. By tearing down the walls that separate the causes and consequences of climate change we can force a more honest reckoning with reality. Once the victims of climate change have the right to seek refuge in Europe and North America, it will obliterate the moral hazard of global warming. As rich nations finally start to feel the heat, so to speak, you can bet they'll act fast, doing everything in their power to ensure that people's home regions remain livable. Even if it means pushing for a new, more ecological, economic model.

This might seem unrealistic at a time of rising anti-immigrant sentiment. But either we do it now, finding orderly ways to integrate climate refugees and allowing ourselves to be spurred to action by the suffering we're forced to confront, or down the road, we're going to face a refugee crisis more severe, violent and destabilising than anything we can imagine. We have a choice.

6

The New Refugees

Nicole Alzapiedi

Nicole Alzapiedi is an intern at the Heinrich Böll Foundation, a political foundation affiliated with the German Green Party and named after the Nobel Prize-winning novelist Heinrich Böll.

One of the defining features of post-war border policy has been the opening of borders to refugees per the terms of the Convention Relating to the Status of Refugees, which was signed shortly after the end of World War II in 1951. But, as Nicole Alzapiedi writes, a refugee system established by the United Nations in 1951 is not equipped to handle the most prevalent cause of displacement in the twenty-first century: the groups of people fleeing their homelands near the equator due to the effects of climate change.

While the mass movement of people fleeing war-torn Syria is widely recognized as a refugee crisis, the growing number of men, women and children fleeing Central America are more often labeled as economic migrants. In fact, a vast majority are fleeing extreme levels of violence in their communities, from gangs, or at the hands of human traffickers. Yet, this does not necessarily qualify migrants for refugee status under the framework of the 1951 Refugee Convention. Yet, despite the differences in the two crises, an important contributing factor in both migration movements is actually the same: climate change.

"The Correlation between Climate Change and Migration: From the Margins to the Mainstream?" by Nicole Alzapiedi, Heinrich-Böll-Stiftung Washington, DC, May 31, 2019. Reprinted by permission.

Climate change is increasingly becoming a top political priority for global policymakers. One of the first acts proposed by the newest United States House of Representatives was the Green New Deal, an ambitious plan to fight climate change, but one that failed to mention climate-induced migration. While referencing provisions for "frontline and vulnerable communities," the proposal does not include any measures for those who are forced to migrate due to climate change. Similarly, while the majority of Syrians coming to Europe have qualified for refugee status, the EU has not put in place legal measures to adequately deal with climate migrants from the Sahel region. The Joint Africa-EU strategy that came out of the Africa-EU summit in 2007 does address the need for a common migration policy, as well as to fight illegal migration and human trafficking, but fails to mention climate migration from Africa to the EU. Yet solutions to the growing challenge of climate migration are urgently needed.

Climate Change Exacerbated the Syrian Crisis

Climate change was an important contributing factor to the Syrian conflict in 2011 and the subsequent refugee crisis. Syria lies in the Fertile Crescent, a region considered the birthplace of agriculture, urbanization, writing, science, and trade, which was plentiful in rich and fertile soils that were watered by the Tigris, Euphrates, Nile and Jordan rivers. Yet this "birthplace of agriculture" has, in recent decades, experienced some of its worst droughts in history. As a report published by the Environmental Justice Foundation noted, between 1999 and 2011 Syria experienced two of its worst droughts in history, which resulted in major crop failures. The first occurred in 1999 and caused the barley crop production to drop to less than half of the previous year, leaving nearly 30,000 people food vulnerable. In the period between 2006 and 2011, between 1.3 and 1.5 million Syrians were forced to migrate from their farms due to drought. What followed was an influx of people into the already economically poor cities of Syria, including Aleppo, Damascus, Dara'a, Hama and Homs. According to a World Bank report of 2014, by 2011, 82.5% of Syrians used migration as an "adaptation strategy" in response to the droughts in Syria. The report noted that the increased migration into urban areas led to more unemployment in these already struggling cities, while the lack of action by the Assad regime to help alleviate these pressures contributed to growing political unrest. In the words of Former Secretary of Defense Chuck Hagel, climate change functioned as a "threat multiplier," exacerbating tensions and helping to precipitate the ensuing conflict.

Droughts Across Central America Are Driving Migration

Syria is not a unique case in which the consequences of climate change led to migration. In 2018 and 2019, the United States/Mexico border saw a significant influx of migrants from Central America that is likely also linked to environmental factors. In Central America, there is a strip of land called the Dry Corridor, which stretches through Honduras, Guatemala, Nicaragua, and El Salvador. The area frequently experiences irregular rainfall and seasons of extreme drought followed by heavy rainfalls. Farmers in the Dry Corridor had developed strategies over centuries to cope with the dry land. However, more recently, climate change has made the land nearly impossible to cultivate. A UN report from 2016 noted that the Dry Corridor experienced its worst drought in ten years, leaving 3.5 million people in need of humanitarian assistance. In a region where the economy is highly dependent on agriculture, one bad season of a crop can have a deep impact on the livelihood of local residents. For example, 14 percent of the Honduran economy, and 21 percent of the economy of El Salvador is dependent on agriculture. One of the greatest crops affected in recent years has been the coffee crop, which is also one of the four largest exported crops from Central America. NPR reported that in recent years, 70% of the farms producing coffee plants in the region were affected by the drought, and 1.7 million people lost their jobs in the coffee industry. As a result of this devastation many people decided to leave their land and find work elsewhere. Those who leave can accurately be described as economic migrants, because they are no longer able to make a living from their land. Yet, the underlying problem is that climate change has made their land unsuitable for agriculture.

Farmers Are Displaced Across the Sahel

A growing body of research suggests that climate change is also an underlying factor in migration both within Africa and from Africa to Europe. Just like farmers in Syria and Central America, farmers in the Sahel Belt of Africa are struggling to continue traditional agricultural activities under increasingly erratic climate conditions. The most affected countries include Northern Nigeria, Chad, Niger and Mali. A UN report of 2013 shows that these countries are experiencing their worst droughts in history and that over 80% of the region's land is degraded. Similar to the cases of Syria and Central America there is a population that is heavily dependent on rain-fed agriculture and no longer able to make a living off of the land. People are forced to leave their homes and about 10% attempt to migrate to Europe.

Climate Migrants Need International Legal Protection

As it stands today, there is no internationally binding legal framework to protect the rights of climate migrants across international borders. The UN 1951 Refugee Convention defines a refugee as having a "well founded fear of being persecuted for reasons of race, religion, nationality, membership of a particular social group or political opinion, is outside the country of his nationality and is unable or, owing to such fear, is unwilling to avail himself of the protection of that country; or who, not having a nationality and being outside the country of his former habitual residence as a result of such events, is unable or, owing to such fear, is unwilling to return to it." Although there is a growing call to develop new legal frameworks for climate migrants, or climate "refugees" as they are sometimes called, it has most often led to initiatives or conventions with non-binding resolutions. Relief programs are generally designed to help people after a natural disaster or major incident has occurred, but there are no international preemptive measures in place for regions that are severely affected by climate change already.

As climate change increasingly becomes a global policy priority (the recent European Parliament elections have been described as the "climate elections"), there is a new awareness of the need to incorporate climate-induced migration into international legal frameworks in order to better and more proactively address it. The Global Compact for Migration, signed in December 2018, for the first time mentioned climate change as a key factor in migration. Prior to this, there have been a few significant instruments created which reference to climate refugees. The Kampala Convention, which was adopted by the African Union and implemented in 2012, is the first legally binding document in the world which obliges states to protect internally displaced persons (IDPs), including those displaced by natural or man-made disasters. Although an improvement, the Convention still only applies to internal displacement within the states of the African Union. This means that African states are obliged to help persons displaced within their own borders due to climate change, but there is no legal obligation to help those crossing international borders. The UN has also hosted multiple human rights and environmental conventions where the topic of climate refugees and displaced persons have been discussed, without agreeing on legally enforceable instruments.

Growing Awareness About the Victims of Climate Change

Mainstream news outlets are increasingly drawing attention to climate migration. *The New York Times*, *Washington Post*, and *The Guardian* have all reported on climate change as an underlying factor of the migrant caravans from Central America. There is also a growing body of scholarly articles on climate change as a factor in the Syrian civil war. In civil society, one of the organizations that has tried to bring the issue of climate migration into the public debate is the Nansen Initiative, which came out of the Nansen Conference on Climate Change and Displacement in Oslo in 2011. The initiative, led by Norway and Switzerland, aims to address cross-border challenges that have arisen due to climate change, including climate refugees. The International Organization of Migration has also outlined policies to address the correlation between migration, climate change and the environment.

Yet the most promising momentum is at the grassroots. Movements like the Sunrise Movement, which inspired Congresswoman Alexandria Ocasio Cortez's Green New Deal, or the student-led "Fridays for Future" movement sparked by the teenage activist Greta Thunberg have succeeded in drawing global attention to the climate crisis. They have had far more success than traditional policy initiatives in overcoming entrenched political interests and advocating for the rights of affected communities. So far, these prominent movements have failed to connect the climate crisis to some of its most vulnerable victims: the poorest farmers forced to abandon their land in Honduras, in Niger, or Syria. Yet it is precisely these people who bear the brunt of the climate crisis and who need a movement to advocate for their rights.

7

Transnational Refugee Nation

Peter Beaumont

Peter Beaumont is a journalist for the Guardian *and a winner of the Orwell Prize, the Amnesty National Press Award, and the Webby Award. He is the author of* The Secret Life of War: Journeys Through Modern Conflict.

Just how many people in the world live between borders? Peter Beaumont writes about the 16.2 million people who were forced to flee their homes in 2017, asserting that while the numbers are unprecedented, institutions are falling into place to accommodate a new transborder population. This population exists inside the borders of nations around the world, but their presence is understood to only be temporary. However, their time in these liminal spaces could last years, decades, or even lifetimes.

The number of people forced to flee their homes rose to a record high in 2017, with 16.2 million people newly displaced around the world. The figure includes people who have been displaced for the first time, and those who have been forced from their homes multiple times.

The figure of 68.5 million displaced people—3 million higher than the total population of the UK—includes 25.4 million refugees, 40 million internally displaced and 3.1 million asylum seekers.

"Record 68.5 million people fleeing war or persecution worldwide," by Peter Beaumont, Guardian News and Media Ltd, June 19, 2018. Reprinted by permission.

The increase came despite the return of more than 5 million displaced people to their countries of origins.

The annual figures, compiled by the UN refugee agency, UNHCR, saw five countries accounting for two-thirds of all refugees (excluding those defined as long-term Palestinian refugees): Syria (6.3 million); Afghanistan (2.6 million); South Sudan (2.4 million); Myanmar (1.2 million) and Somalia (986,400).

The new figures emerged after the actor and director Angelina Jolie, a special envoy for the UN agency, warned of a funding shortfall for the agency's work in Syria—the largest group of displaced.

Speaking during a visit to Domiz Camp in Iraq on Sunday, home to 33,000 refugees displaced by the Syrian war, Jolie told a press conference that the agency's appeal for Syrian refugees was hugely underfunded even in comparison with last year.

"When UNHCR's Syria response was only 50% funded last year, and this year it is only 17% funded, there are terrible human consequences. We should be under no illusions about this. When there is even not the bare minimum of aid, refugee families cannot receive adequate medical treatment," Jolie said. "Women and girls are left vulnerable to sexual violence, many children cannot go to school, and we squander the opportunity of being able to invest in refugees so that they can acquire new skills and support their families."

The new totals come at the end of a decade of sharply rising numbers of displaced, which have risen inexorably from more than 42 million in 2007 to the current total. This means one in every 110 people in the world is currently displaced, with most of the sharp increase occurring in the last five years.

Although Syria once again dominated the figures, 2017 was also marked by a significant rise in displaced people from North and Central America, with increasing numbers of people journeying to seek asylum in Mexico and the US, even as Venezuelans continued to flow out to neighbouring countries.

Bucking the depressing global trends, however, crossings of the eastern Mediterranean decreased compared with 2016.

The totals also saw the sixth successive year of increases in the number of refugees under UNHCR's mandate, with a rise of just under 3 million last year to a total just short of 20 million, the highest known total to date.

"As in previous years, Syria continued to account for the largest forcibly displaced population globally," states the report.

"As of the end of 2017, there were 12.6 million forcibly displaced Syrians, comprising around 6.3 million refugees, 146,700 asylum-seekers, and 6.2 million IDPs [displaced people].

"The situations in the Democratic Republic of the Congo [DRC] and Myanmar deteriorated rapidly in the second half of 2017, affecting millions of people.

"The flight of refugees from Myanmar to Bangladesh occurred at a particularly rapid rate. Over 2017, 655,500 arrived in Bangladesh, mainly concentrated in 100 days from the end of August, making the humanitarian response very challenging. In addition, there was a large proportion of infants, children and pregnant women among refugees and IDPs from the DRC and Myanmar, adding a further layer of complexity for interventions.

The UN High Commissioner for Refugees, Filippo Grandi, said: "We are at a watershed, where success in managing forced displacement globally requires a new and far more comprehensive approach so that countries and communities aren't left dealing with this alone.

"But there is reason for some hope. Fourteen countries are already pioneering a new blueprint for responding to refugee situations and in a matter of months a new Global Compact on Refugees will be ready for adoption by the United Nations General Assembly.

"Today, on the eve of World Refugee Day, my message to member states is: please support this. No one becomes a refugee by choice; but the rest of us can have a choice about how we help."

Matthew Saltmarsh, a spokesperson for UNHCR, underlined the worrying trends.

"What we are seeing in this data is overall displacement at an unprecedented high six years in a row," he said. "In terms of refugee numbers it is the largest increase in a single year."

8

The American Example

Jacob G. Hornberger

Jacob G. Hornberger is the founder and president of the Future of Freedom Foundation, a libertarian organization that aims to advance an uncompromising case for libertarianism in both foreign and domestic policy.

The United States, Jacob G. Hornberger writes, represents one of the most successful examples of what a world with open borders might look like. A collection of former colonies that considered themselves disparate domains before the American Revolution, the free flow of people and goods between the colonies created a common culture and one of the most powerful economies in the world. Furthermore, it established a moral philosophy opposed to the idea of keeping people out.

The American people are extremely fortunate. Two hundred years ago, their Founding Fathers used the Constitution to prohibit American government officials from ever enacting trade and immigration restrictions between the respective states of the Union. This meant that the citizens of any state could buy and sell goods and services with the citizens of any other state, without tariffs or import restrictions. It also meant that citizens of one state could travel or move to another state without permission, passport, or other restriction.

"The Case for Unilateral Free Trade and Open Immigration," by Jacob G. Hornberger, The Future of Freedom Foundation, November 1, 1994. Reprinted by permission.

Most American politicians and bureaucrats today honestly believe that free trade and open immigration are harmful to a society. Therefore, if today's government officials were not prohibited by the Constitution from enacting trade and immigration controls between the respective states, life in the United States would be dramatically different. Each state would enact a host of import restrictions, tariffs, and immigration controls to protect the citizenry from "foreigners" and "foreign goods" from other parts of the country.

For example, the state of Georgia would impose import quotas on goods from Florida. Why? Because there is a trade imbalance between the two states—that is, Georgians are purchasing more from Floridians than Floridians are purchasing from Georgians. There would be trade negotiations and trade summits between the governors of the two states, as they tried to negotiate the trade imbalance between their respective states. If the negotiations failed, a trade war between Georgia and Florida would ensue.

Another example, the state of Texas would impose strict immigration controls restricting the immigration into Texas of those weird New Yorkers. After all, there is a high unemployment rate in Texas and, therefore, the Texas economy could not absorb an additional inflow of people. Moreover, an influx of New Yorkers would cause wages in Texas to drop—and the New Yorkers emigrating to Texas would take jobs away from Texans.

Kansas would impose immigration controls on California, because the latter has a much higher incidence of AIDS cases. "We can't permit free immigration from California," the Kansas officials would say, "because we might get inundated by AIDS patients."

Fortunately, due to the wisdom and foresight of Americans two hundred years ago, these types of restrictions cannot be imposed by American politicians and bureaucrats today. And make no mistake about it—the *only* reason they are not imposed is because the Constitution does now allow their imposition. Without these constitutional restrictions, American politicians and bureaucrats, being firmly committed to the idea of trade and immigration controls—and being so subject to the pressures, influences, and financial contributions of special-interest groups—and believing that trade and immigration restrictions are the key to economic prosperity—would riddle American society with them.

It is impossible to overstate the importance and benefits Americans have in living in what is the largest free-trade and free-immigration zone in the world. We travel across state boundaries and never see a customs or immigration official. In fact, the usual way we know we are in a different state is that we see a road sign that says: "Welcome to the state of . . . ." We buy and sell goods across state lines without ever concerning ourselves with whether we are violating some type of tariff or import or export control—or with whether we are alleviating or aggravating some trade imbalance with another state.

And it is this principle—the principle of free trade and open immigration within the fifty states—that is one of the major reasons that the American people have—and have had—the highest standard of living in history.

For standards of living of people can rise through the mere act of exchange!

For example, suppose you have ten apples and I have ten oranges. I value one of your oranges more than my tenth apple; and you value one of my apples more than your tenth orange. We trade—one apple for one orange. Our standard of living has improved—through the mere act of exchange! Thus, the more people are free to trade, the higher the standards of living tend to be.

And the same principle applies internationally—when people are free to trade and travel—whether it is with people of another state, another city, or another nation—they are able to improve their standards of living.

Then, why have American government officials (despite their apparent devotion to freedom) imposed a strangulating set of import restrictions and tariffs on the goods and services coming into the U.S.? And why have they tightly restricted the flow of people traveling or moving to the U.S.?

The reason lies in politics and special-interest groups.

Consider the following example. Suppose a Toyota is priced at $15,000. A Chevrolet Impala, let us say, sells for the same price. You, as a consumer, decide that you like the quality of the Toyota better. You decide to buy the Toyota.

General Motors screams to the U.S. government: "Force Mary to buy from General Motors." Union workers chime in: "Mary's purchase of a Toyota will take our jobs away." Government officials bow under the pressure. They do not force Mary to buy the Impala. But they say to Mary: "If you buy the Toyota, you pay $15,000 to Toyota and a $5,000 tariff (tax) to the U.S. government." If Mary buys the Chevrolet, her standard of living—from her perspective—is not as high as it could have been. If she buys the Toyota, the government has, in effect, legally stolen the sum of $5,000 from her; and her standard of living has dropped by $5,000.

The worst part of it is that the people who pay the biggest price for tariffs and import restrictions are the poor, because these taxes are regressive—that is, their weight falls disproportionately greater on poor people. In other words, the same government that professes to have such a big concern for the poor with its welfare state, impoverishes the poor through trade restrictions for the sake of wealthy special-interest groups.

Consider immigration controls. There are good and honorable people from the Republic of Mexico today sitting in American penitentiaries along the Mexican border. Their crime? Trying to enter into a trade with an American—a trade by which both of their standards of living would be improved. The Mexican wants to work, and an American wants to hire him. But the same government that "loves" the poor with its welfare state, slams the jailhouse door on the poor who have committed the heinous American crime of trying to improve their lives through labor.

Consider the Haitian people. Using its political and military power to control international trade, the U.S. government has imposed a trade embargo on the Haitian people—using force to prevent goods and services from reaching Haiti, which, in turn, has caused death and destitution from starvation. Then, when the Haitian people attempt to survive by trying to escape to the U.S., American government officials capture them and forcibly return them to the death and destitution that awaits them. In other words, despite its supposed devotion to the poor through the welfare state, the U.S. government, through its powers over trade and immigration, condemns thousands of the poorest people in the world to death and destitution.

The ultimate argument against trade and immigration controls, however, lies not in economic terms—that is, that free trade and open immigration result in higher standards of living. The real argument lies in moral principles. A person has the right to do what he wants with his own money. He has a right to buy anything he wishes from whoever wishes to sell to him. He has a right to sell what belongs to him to whoever wishes to buy it. He has a right to employ anyone he wishes, so long as the employee wants to work there. He has a right to work for anyone, so long as the employer wants him to work there. Individuals have a right to travel and trade—whether domestically or internationally—without interference from government officials.

What should be the trade and immigration policy of the United States—and, for that matter, all other nations? To unilaterally drop —without negotiations, agreements, or treaties—all trade and immigration controls. This would mean that Americans, upon returning from an overseas trip, would return to the U.S. in the same way they return to Dallas from San Francisco—without ever waiting in a line to see a customs or immigration official. It would also mean that people all over the world could simply get on a plane and travel to Minneapolis or New York or Memphis, also without ever having to see a customs or immigration official. It would mean that businessmen all over the world could buy from Americans and sell to Americans the same way that Texans buy from and sell to Virginians.

What is the response of the "controllers" to a world of free trade and open immigration?

"They'll go on welfare." Well, one solution is to end the dole for everyone, including Americans. Alternatively, immigrants are not citizens; therefore, there is no requirement that they be permitted to be on the dole. Thus, if "no dole" was an express condition of immigration, immigrants who would come to the U.S. would be the types we want—people who like to take risks, work hard, and be self-reliant and independent—energizing qualities that every society should cherish.

"They'll enter our public schools." Then, prohibit them from doing so. The result would be that they will form their own private, independent schools—and, consequently, provide the nucleus of a new type of person in America: an independent thinker who loves knowledge for its own sake, unlike the public-school student, who simply learns how to memorize and obey.

"They'll take jobs away from Americans." Every American who works today does so under the assumption that he can be replaced with a worker who has moved from another state. All that open immigration would do is open the market even more. But with one big benefit—the new spending by immigrants would open up a wealth of new employment opportunities in the businesses that would have to open or expand to meet the new economic demands.

"They'll dump their products on Americans." Then, retaliate by dumping your products on Americans or on foreigners—consumers will love it! More important, when a person opens a business, he does so under certain risks. One of these risks is that someone else might satisfy the consumers better than other sellers—and that this might happen through low prices or even free goods being given to consumers. If a businessman does not want to take that risk, then he should not go into business.

"They'll get their governments to subsidize their reduced goods." Again, this is a risk that exists in the business world, even domestically. Unfortunately, we live in a world in which people permit their governments to plunder them in order to give a dole to others, including businessmen. No one forces someone to open a business. If a person does not want to take the risk of a government giving a competitor a dole, then there is a simple solution: do not open the business.

"Millions of people will immediately move to the United States." Perhaps. But we must first keep in mind that U.S. government import restrictions create miserable economic conditions in many countries that encourage people to want to emigrate. Once those restrictions are lifted, there is a probability that with the increased economic prosperity in foreign countries, many would-be emigrants would choose to stay at home among friends and family. But if millions did come, great! History has shown that cheap labor, like cheap goods, is a tremendous economic boon to the people of a society. Give us your tired, huddled masses yearning to breathe free—and watch economic prosperity here soar!

Trade restrictions and immigration restrictions are one of the most abominable features of American society today. They have brought impoverishment to millions of poor people—both domestic and foreign. And they violate one of the most fundamental precepts of a free society—the right to do what you want with your money and your life. The times call for leadership—and the American people should lead the world by forcing their government officials to unilaterally lift all trade and immigration controls—and, ultimately, by constitutionally prohibiting American government officials from ever imposing them again.

9

A History of Passports, Nationalism, and Borders

John Torpey

John Torpey is a professor of sociology and history and director of the Ralph Bunche Institute for International Studies at the Graduate Center, City University of New York.

In this day and age, it is taken for granted that one must have a passport to travel between countries. However, this was not always the case. Free movement was restricted in the early twentieth century because most countries were authoritarian or colonial, and before that it was restricted because forced labor was common throughout much of Europe and America and the loss of labor had to be prevented. It is only since the mid-twentieth century that movement became free enough to cause concern, and nations responded by creating restrictions on who could enter their borders.

The U.S. State Department has been denying passports to U.S. citizens who live in Texas near the U.S.-Mexico border since the George W. Bush administration, according to news reports.

Specifically, the government is denying passports to people delivered by midwives in Texas's Rio Grande Valley as well as people delivered by midwives in Mexico. The midwives are believed to have falsified U.S. birth certificates for those born in Mexico.

"How passports evolved to help governments regulate your movement," by John Torpey, The Conversation, September 7, 2018, https://theconversation.com/how-passports-evolved-to-help-governments-regulate-your-movement-101657. Licensed under CC BY-ND 4.0 International.

The denials, though begun under the Bush Administration, continued with the Obama and Trump administrations. And critics say they are part of a tide of anti-immigrant measures that includes other Trump administration efforts to restrict entry to the U.S. Those measures range from the travel ban on Muslims from certain countries entering the U.S. to White House proposals to develop a merit-based immigration system.

Meanwhile, the entry of thousands of immigrants and refugees into Europe in recent years has generated a populist backlash against outsiders.

These developments raise fundamental questions about migration from country to country: When and how did governments get the power to limit people's movements? And how did passports come to play such a crucial role?

I explored these questions in the research I did for my book, "The Invention of the Passport." I believe this history can help us understand how governments have assumed so much control over where people can go.

Moving Around

Throughout much of European and American history, labor was forced. Both landowners and states sought to restrict the movement of slaves and serfs in order to prevent the loss of their labor forces. Before the 19th century, however, their ability to keep people from leaving was tenuous and a major source of concern for their owners. In the United States, patrols helped enforce fugitive slave laws, but their reach was limited.

Nobles, merchants and free peasants may have moved about freely, but could be shut in or out of a city in an emergency if the gates were closed.

Until fairly recently, stopping people from leaving a plantation or farm was more important to governments than keeping people from coming in, at least during peaceful times.

That changed following the French Revolution, which began in 1789. Nationalism—the idea that particular "peoples" or "nations" should govern themselves—became a powerful force in Europe and, gradually, around the world. By the middle of the 19th century, both U.S. slavery and European serfdom declined as a result of rising notions of "free labor" and the desire to make populations feel a sense of belonging to the country. The shift toward free, mobile labor meant people had more opportunity than ever to move around.

There were major exceptions: By the early 20th century, the overwhelming majority of states in the world were still authoritarian or colonial. People who lived there could not freely move about.

However, after World War II and the gradual breakup of colonial empires, moving within countries came to be widely understood as a matter of individual freedom. Such movement facilitated the ability of laborers to go where they were needed, and thus tended to be supported by governments.

People leaving a country might still have been regulated by their government in the post-war era. But this became less of a concern because democracy spread. More democratic countries were less worried about people leaving than were those that forced their populations to stay and work, such as those "behind the Iron Curtain."

It was control over the entry of outsiders that became paramount with the mid-20th-century triumph of nation-states. Foreigners, the thinking goes, might not have the interests of "the people" at heart. A kind of permanent suspicion took hold in which foreigners were deemed ineligible for entry without evidence that they would not become troublesome. Possession of a passport helped promote that by showing who a person was and where they could be sent if they proved undesirable.

As I argue in my book, this transformation in regulating movement created a new world that would be largely unrecognizable to those who lived before World War I. Governments everywhere now restrict during peacetime the entry of people they deem "undesirable" on criminal, ethnic, economic, medical and demographic grounds.

Meanwhile, movement within countries loosened up, although particular spaces—such as military bases, prisons and areas containing valued resources—often remain off limits to many.

Since then, crossing international borders has become the big challenge for people wishing to move. Passports became key to regulating this process.

Papers, Please

Passports, seemingly modest documents, were introduced gradually in many places in the modern world. In the United States, the federal government in 1856 asserted the exclusive right to issue passports and mandated that they be issued only to U.S. citizens.

Once simple pieces of paper, passports have evolved into standardized booklets that identify persons and tell governments where they should be sent if they are deemed inadmissible—their fundamental purpose in international law.

Today, passports are perceived mainly as documents that are used to constrain entry into a country, weeding out the relatively rare individual who might be a criminal, a terrorist or someone otherwise at odds with the receiving government's preferences.

Since the 9/11 terrorist attacks, governments have developed a greater interest in technological means of identifying border-crossers. For example, governments that belong to the standard-setting International Civil Aviation Organization have developed machine-readable passports with encrypted identification information, making them harder for anyone to use other than the actual bearer.

Those whose movements are being scrutinized so intently today in North America and Europe are from countries whose citizens are often regarded as undesirable due to poverty, culture, religion or other attributes. Entry of these outsiders has generated a wave of support for nationalist, populist parties that are upending the traditional openness to foreigners in the United States and fuelling xenophobia in Europe.

By challenging the passport applications of people born near the Mexican border, the Trump administration is also reminding us that passports are a reflection of one's citizenship. Without one, you can't leave the country and count on being able to return. Their freedom to remain in the U.S. is at risk.

We live in a world in which the entry of those who are deemed "desireable" is greatly facilitated, while that of those deemed "undesirable" is greatly constrained. Freedom of movement into other countries is a reliable expectation only for those from the rich world with no blemishes on their records; for the rest, crossing borders can be very difficult, indeed.

10

An Economic Argument Against Open Borders

Paul Ormerod

Paul Ormerod is an economist and the director of Volterra Consulting, a firm that specializes in the economics of transport and property development.

A logical consequence of the opening of borders around the world has been the increase in economic migration, which some say has dramatically changed the economies of the countries that have been on the receiving end of these movements. Among the most cited economic changes caused by migration is the depression of wages in these countries, which follows the expansion of a labor base to include newcomers. In a market economy, more people means less competition and, it follows, less pay.

Mass immigration increases inequality. This is the unpalatable fact the liberal left in Britain refuses to accept. Markets are imperfect instruments. But it is not necessary to subscribe to free market economic theory to believe that large increases in supply tend to drive down the price. And the price of labour is the wage.

Last Friday, the *Guardian* front page carried a report from the Office for Budget Responsibility, claiming that higher net immigration increased the UK's economic growth rate. According to the mainstream theory of economic growth, this is undoubtedly

"Open borders or fair wages: the left needs to make up its mind," by Paul Ormerod, Guardian News and Media Limited, March 24, 2015. Reprinted by permission.

true. Higher growth can be created by sustained increases of either capital or labour.

But underlying the theory is the assumption that supply and demand balance in these markets, that the prices of the inputs are set at levels such that all available capital or labour is in fact employed and does not remain idle. So this "flourishing modern economy" with high immigration celebrated by the *Guardian* is based on persistent large wage inequalities.

A powerful force in the global economy is driving the increase in inequality that has been seen in western economies over the past few decades. In essence, there has been a massive increase in the effective supply of labour. Over the past three decades or so, China and India have gradually been absorbed into the network of international trade.

This puts pressure on European labour markets. Many call centres, for example, have been relocated to India. But much of the impact of this is indirect, operating via trade flows, and is only really felt by certain sectors of western economies.

Closer to home, the opening up of eastern Europe in the early 1990s has had a strong effect, especially on countries that are their immediate neighbours, such as Germany. Employers soon realised that economies such as Poland and the Czech Republic possessed educated labour forces, whose productivity potential had been suppressed by the gross inefficiencies inherent in planned economies. German companies opened up new production plants in the old Soviet bloc countries in Europe, rather than at home.

The impact on wage rates of this increase in competition was dramatic. Christian Dustmann at University College London has provided clear evidence on the evolution of wage rates in the former West Germany. The 15th percentile of the wage distribution is the level at which only 15% of wages are lower. In West Germany, at the 15th percentile, real wages have fallen almost continuously since the mid-1990s. At the 50th percentile, where half get more and half get less, the reduction has been less sharp.

But the fall had set in by the early 2000s. At the 85th percentile, the mirror image of the 15th, real wages grew strongly, reaping the benefits of the recovery of the economy created by the increase in competitiveness.

It is against this background that New Labour opened up Britain's borders in the late 1990s. It was a major betrayal of the very people the party purported to represent.

In addition to the global competition from countries such as China, in addition to competition closer to home from the economies of eastern Europe, New Labour allowed direct competition to enter the UK labour market on a scale unprecedented in our history.

Not surprisingly, the distribution of wage rates has evolved in very similar ways to those of West Germany. It is the relatively unskilled in the bottom half of the distribution who have lost out. The liberal elite do not suffer.

Indeed, they benefit because many of the services they consume are provided at lower prices than would have been the case without mass immigration. It is sometimes argued that immigrants do jobs that native British workers are unwilling to take.

Very well then, without mass immigration, employers would be obliged to raise the real wage rate to induce these people to take the jobs.

The effects of this extend to benefit levels. With at least half the population facing at best stagnant and often falling real wages, basic political economy requires benefits to be squeezed as well. Hostility to benefits is strongest precisely in the bottom part of the wage distribution. It is political suicide to increase real benefits in this context, regardless of who is in power.

In the so-called neoclassical growth theory of economics, whether of the pre- or post-endogenous variety, by far the most important source of sustained growth is innovation. The age structure of immigration means that it does make a change to per capita economic growth, but one that is barely perceptible.

Moreover, immigrants themselves age eventually, so eventually even this tiny benefit disappears.

A truly modern economy does not rely on more and more capital and labour being fuelled into the machinery of production. That was the old Soviet model.

A modern economy relies instead on innovation. This should be the focus of policy. The potential gains are huge, not marginal and ephemeral.

11

An Economic Argument for Open Borders

Nick Srnicek

Nick Srnicek is a lecturer in international political economy at the City University of London. His research focuses on post-work politics and social reproduction.

According to Nick Srnicek, research by economists overwhelmingly indicates that opening borders would improve wages and quality of life for workers from around the world. Since workers in poorer countries are not provided the same economic and educational opportunities as those in wealthier countries, allowing them to seek work in these wealthier countries would provide them with new and improved opportunities. Opening borders would also benefit workers in more affluent countries, as they are currently forced to compete with workers in poorer countries who must work for lower wages. Eliminating this competition would mean higher wages for all.

I n an ideal world, we would all be able to freely move wherever we wanted. The basic right of people to escape from war, persecution and poverty would be accepted as a given, and no one would have their life determined by their place of birth.

But we don't live in this world, and national borders continue to block the freedom of people to move. Around the world, protectionism is on the rise, as people are told to blame outsiders for threatening their way of life and, more importantly, stealing their jobs.

There is, however, an overwhelming case for open borders that can be made even in the traditionally self-interested language of economics. In fact, our best estimates are that opening the world's borders could increase global GDP by US$100 trillion.

That's US$100,000,000,000,000,000

It sounds like a crazy idea, particularly when the media is dominated by stories about the need to control immigration and the right-wing tabloids trumpet "alternative facts" about how immigration hurts our economies. But every piece of evidence we have says that ending borders would be the single easiest way to improve the living standards of workers around the world—including those in wealthy countries.

The argument is simple enough and has been made by more than one economist. Workers in poorer economies make less than they should. If they were to have all of the benefits of rich countries—advanced education, the latest workplace technologies, and all the necessary infrastructure—these workers would produce and earn as much as their rich country counterparts. What keeps them in poverty is their surroundings. If they were able to pick up and move to more productive areas, they would see their incomes increase many times over.

This means that opening borders is, by a massive amount, the easiest and most effective way to tackle global poverty. Research shows that alternative approaches—for instance, microcredit, higher education standards, and anti-sweatshop activism—all produce lifetime economic gains that would be matched in weeks by open borders. Even small reductions in the barriers posed by borders would bring massive benefits for workers.

Gains for All

Of course, the immediate fear of having open borders is that it will increase competition for jobs and lower wages for those living in rich countries. This misses the fact that globalisation means competition already exists between workers worldwide— under conditions that harm their pay and security. UK workers in manufacturing or IT, for instance, are already competing with low-wage workers in India and Vietnam. Workers in rich countries are already losing, as companies eliminate good jobs and move their factories and offices elsewhere.

Under these circumstances, the function of borders is to keep workers trapped in low-wage areas that companies can freely exploit. Every worker—whether from a rich country or a poor country—suffers as a result. Ending borders would mean an end to this type of competition between workers. It would make us all better off.

The European Union has provided a natural experiment in what happens when borders between rich and poor countries are opened up. And the evidence here is unambiguous: the long-run effects of open borders improve the conditions and wages of all workers. However, in the short-run, some groups (particularly unskilled labourers) can be negatively affected.

The fixes for this are exceedingly simple though. A shortening of the work week would reduce the amount of work supplied, spread the work out more equally among everyone, and give more power to workers—not to mention, more free time to everyone. And the strengthening and proper enforcement of labour laws would make it impossible for companies to hyper-exploit migrant workers. The overall impacts of more workers are exceedingly small in the short-run, and exceedingly positive in the long-run.

As it stands, borders leave workers stranded and competing against each other. The way the global economy is set up is based entirely on competition. This makes us think that potential allies are irreconcilable enemies. The real culprits, however, are businesses that pick up and leave at the drop of a hat, that fire long-time workers in favour of cheaper newcomers, and that break labour laws outright, in order to boost their profits.

Borders leave us as strangers rather than allies. Yet this need not be the case, and as a principle guiding political action, the abolition of borders would rank among the greatest of human achievements.

12

The Political Effects of Open Borders

Anna Maria Mayda and Giovanni Peri

Anna Maria Mayda is an associate professor in the School of Foreign Service and in the department of economics at Georgetown University. Giovanni Peri is the chair of the department of economics at the University of California, Davis.

In a 2018 study, the Cato Institute—a libertarian think tank—argued that immigration patterns in the US have a significant impact on voting outcomes. Support for opening the country's borders to more immigrants followed the arrival of immigrants, while the regions most opposed to opening borders largely came from the parts of the country where the fewest immigrants made up the population. This is notably different from Europe, where studies have found that popular resentment toward immigrants increased in the areas that experienced an influx of immigration.

Political leaders' positions on the issue of immigration can be an important determinant of their electoral success or failure. Immigration took center stage in the 2016 U.S. presidential election and its aftermath, as now-president Donald Trump took strong stands on illegal immigration, the construction of a border wall, refugees from Syria, and "sanctuary cities." The Brexit vote in the United Kingdom and recent political elections in Germany (2017) and Italy (2018) have highlighted the controversial political role of

"The Political Impact of Immigration: Evidence from the United States," by Anna Maria Mayda and Giovanni Peri, Cato Institute, September 12, 2018. Reprinted by permission.

immigration and the electoral success of strong anti-immigration stands. That immigration has an effect on political outcomes has been pointed out in the academic literature. Yet, to our knowledge, no empirical study has looked at the direct connection between election outcomes and immigration in the United States. We tackle this question by analyzing the link between immigration and the vote share received by the Republican Party, across U.S. counties and over time, in the 20-year election cycle between 1990 and 2010.

Three aspects of our analysis are novel. First, we combine economic and demographic data from the U.S. Census and American Community Survey with data on electoral outcomes from the Library of Congress for all types of elections at the U.S. county level. We exploit the large variation in immigration across U.S. counties and time to identify the correlation between immigration and votes for the Republican Party. Second, we focus on the distinction between high-skilled (college-educated) and low-skilled (non-college-educated) immigrants and exploit their differential variation, driven by past networks and differences in skills across countries of origin to separately identify a causal effect of each group. These two types of immigrants affect the economy and labor markets differently and, it turns out, they have very different effects on the votes of U.S. citizens. Third, we allow for heterogeneous effects of high- and low-skilled immigrants on voting outcomes, depending on the economic and demographic characteristics of the receiving county. In analyzing these heterogeneous effects we shed light on the possible mechanisms through which immigration may have impacted the vote share of the Republican Party.

The substantial inflow of immigrants to the United States during the last 30 years has significantly shaped the U.S. economy and society. Immigrants affect native workers' opportunities in the labor market, their productivity, and their specialization. Immigrants can also have an impact on other aspects of the host country's economy (for example, through fiscal effects, consumption, and contributions to scientific innovation), as well as on its culture, social norms, and sense of security. In addition, immigration can affect political outcomes. We analyze the latter outcomes but, in doing so, we also need to take into account the impact of immigration through the other channels. Indeed, we assume that, through their votes, U.S. citizens respond to the perceived economic and psychological costs and benefits—through the labor-market, fiscal, and noneconomic mechanisms—of having more immigrants in their county. We posit that their probability of voting for the Republican Party goes up if the perceived cost of an increase in immigrants (high-skilled or low-skilled) is larger than the perceived benefit. In this simple framework we associate the Republican Party with more restrictive immigration policies, which it usually championed in the 20 years we consider. Immigration may also affect the outcome of elections by extending the pool of voters (i.e., directly) by adding the votes of newly naturalized immigrants. However, we find evidence suggesting that the main effect of immigrants on Republican votes comes from the indirect impact on preferences of existing voters.

Our strongest and most significant finding is that an increase in high-skilled immigrants as a share of the local population is associated with a strong and significant decrease in the vote share for the Republican Party. By contrast, an increase in the low-skilled immigrant share of the population is associated with a strong and significant increase in Republican votes. These effects are common to presidential and House and Senate elections. Combining the two effects, the net impact of the increased immigrant share on the average U.S. county was negative for the Republican Party between 1990 and 2010. This was because immigration in this period was on average college-biased.

The findings described above are average effects across U.S. counties. The perceived costs and benefits of immigrants, however, should differ according to the local characteristics of the county, and the heterogeneous effects across counties should depend on local labor-market characteristics, on the extent of local fiscal redistribution, and on noneconomic characteristics of citizens, consistent with these perceptions. This is indeed what we find. The estimates show that the pro-Republican effect of low-skilled immigrants was particularly strong in counties where the share of unskilled natives was higher, where economic activity was less dense, and where the county was prevalently nonurban. These findings suggest that low-skilled natives and those living in less dynamic and more rural economies are more likely to feel in competition with low-skilled immigrants. At the same time, we find evidence of a pro-Democrat shift in response to high-skilled immigrants in counties where the share of low-skilled natives was large. However, the impact was still significant and pro-Democrat in counties with a large share of high-skilled natives. These findings are consistent with an overall perceived positive effect of high-skilled immigrants on citizens, which is stronger where citizens are unskilled. Overall, these effects are likely to be driven by a combination of labor-market effects based on relationships of complementarity and substitutability and, in the case of high-skilled immigration, positive externalities (for example, through innovation) and positive fiscal effects (through greater tax revenues). This is consistent with empirical evidence that fiscal transfers from highly educated immigrants to natives are positive and that high-skilled workers benefit the local economy and wages.

By providing systematic and robust evidence on the relationship between U.S. immigration and voting outcomes, we are also able to shed light on "conventional wisdom" on the topic and on puzzles in the literature. Anecdotal evidence suggests, and we confirm in our data, that on average immigration in U.S. counties reduces the Republican vote share. Political scientists and analysts seem to read this evidence as driven by a "pro-Democratic Party" direct political effect—the idea that naturalized immigrants vote predominantly for the Democratic Party, which has a pro-immigrant platform—and by the fact that this effect dominates whatever indirect effect immigration has on the way existing voters vote. At first sight, this interpretation may seem consistent with the empirical evidence: an increase in the share of citizen (voting) migrants reduces the

Republican vote share, while an increase in the share of noncitizen migrants has, on average, no effect. However, a closer look suggests that the main impact of immigration on voting outcomes comes from the skill level of immigrants—which affects the voting behavior of existing voters—and not from how naturalized immigrants vote. High-skilled immigrants, both naturalized and not, are associated with a lower share of the Republican vote, and vice versa low-skilled immigrants, naturalized or not, are associated with a higher share of the Republican vote.

Not only is systematic evidence on the link between immigration and election outcomes scarce in the case of the United States, but the little evidence that does exist is puzzling in light of the results found for other countries. For example, several papers on continental European countries find that immigrants increased the electoral vote share of right-wing, anti-immigration parties. What explains the opposite results on the two sides of the Atlantic? Why is the average political impact of immigration (on conservative parties' votes) positive in the case of European countries and negative in the case of the United States? Our analysis shows that the two sets of results are not inconsistent. Immigrants to Europe have been, on average, less skilled than immigrants to the United States, and the local labor force in Europe is also less skilled (lower share of college-educated) than in the United States. Our analysis shows that the local economic conditions of a region together with the skill level of immigrants affect citizens' perceived impact of immigration and their vote response. Specifically, areas with low education levels and low urbanization may be more ready to embrace nationalistic views in response to low-skilled immigrants. This seems as true in the United States as in Europe. It is also in line with the results of the 2016 Brexit referendum in which, following the message of right-wing and antiimmigration parties, most nonurban areas outside of London voted for the United Kingdom to leave the European Union, while the urban, high-skilled, and densely populated region of London voted to stay within the European Union. This can be partly due to the large recent inflow of immigrants to the United Kingdom, which was less skilled in the rural low-skilled areas of England and had a different impact there vis-á-vis the urban high-skilled metropolitan London region.

After estimating the impact of increased immigration on the Republican share of votes, we use these estimates and the recent growth in immigrant populations to see how much of the recent shift of votes toward the Republican Party in the 2012 and 2016 elections was predicted using our empirical model. We find that about 22 percent of the variation in the growth of votes for the Republican Party across U.S. counties can be explained by the estimated marginal effect of immigration in the specification that allows for different skill groups and heterogeneous effects.

13

Open Borders Are Moral Borders

Guy Aitchison

Guy Aitchison received his PhD from University College London (UCL). He has taught at King's College London and UCL while serving as a Max Weber fellow, a project of the European University Institute.

Do people have the right to cross borders? In posing the issue of open borders as a fundamentally moral question, the debate veers away from studies of the political or economic effects of immigration or free trade and asks if countries have any right to stop the free movement of people according to their will. Some writers, Aitchison notes, compare the institution of borders to social relations that are commonly thought of as barbaric now, such as feudalism or slavery. Is one truly free if one's movement is restricted?

I n early December, British foreign secretary Boris Johnson was forced to deny reports that he'd told a group of ambassadors he was personally in favour of the free movement of people across the European Union.

Given his previous negative public statements on the issue, reports of his private support for the principle, which allows all EU citizens to move freely around the bloc, came as a surprise. Speaking to a Czech newspaper in mid-November, he had rubbished the idea that free movement is a central principle of the EU and denied that "every human being has some fundamental God-given right to move wherever they want."

Many were quick to point out that Johnson was confused on a matter of law. The EU parliament's lead Brexit negotiator Guy Verhofstadt quipped on Twitter that he would bring a copy of the 1957 Treaty of Rome, the treaty establishing the European Economic Community (later the EU), to the negotiations to correct Johnson. Article 3 of the treaty proposes the abolition of "obstacles to freedom of movement" between member states.

Yet while Johnson's shaky grip of the facts about the EU should not surprise us, his comments inadvertently touch upon a fundamental moral issue that often gets overlooked in debates around immigration: whether there is a fundamental human right to move.

The Right to Immigrate

Talk of building walls, taking back control and "legitimate concerns" over immigration implicitly assume that states have a right to exclude who they wish. Yet among moral and political philosophers there is no consensus on the legitimacy of border controls and important arguments have been made for a human right to immigrate.

Those who take this position are not necessarily committed to an anarchist perspective that rejects the very idea of states — though free movement was an important demand for radical philosophers linked to what's known as the "alter-globalisation" movement. Instead, some argue for freedom of movement based on the logical and consistent extension of mainstream democratic values.

Under existing international human rights law, Article 13.1 of the Universal Declaration of Human Rights contains a right to freedom of movement for individuals within states, but there is no such right to freedom of movement between states.

We tend to think of the right to free movement within a state as an essential freedom. If the government banned you from visiting and settling in certain parts of the country you would rightly feel outraged. The government would be denying you the choice of where to live and study, who you can form relationships with, who you can associate with on a religious or political basis, and it would be denying you a range of important economic opportunities. These are fundamental choices that affect how our lives are lived.

But notice that these very same considerations also apply to freedom of movement across borders. In today's globalised world, restricting your right to move across borders is not so very different from confining you to the boundaries of Yorkshire, say, or Seattle.

Citizenship In an Age of Growing Inequality

Perhaps the strongest argument, however, concerns the brute injustice of the world's current border regime. Those born into prosperous states enjoy life prospects virtually unknown to would-be migrants in poorer parts of the world who are condemned to lives of poverty and destitution.

This fact seems morally arbitrary if we accept the basic equality of human beings. In the words of the philosopher Joseph Carens, citizenship in Western liberal democracies is: "The modern equivalent of feudal privilege ... an inherited status that greatly enhances one's life chances."

Global inequality has been increasing dramatically over the past few decades. According to World Bank figures, American citizens were 72 times richer than sub-Saharan Africans and 80 times richer than south Asians by the year 2000.

The argument for a right to move is strengthened further when we consider how wealthy, Western states have profited from colonial relationships with many of the very same countries migrants are fleeing. These same states are among those who now set the rules of the global economy to their own advantage thanks to power imbalances in the World Trade Organisation, International Monetary Fund and World Bank.

Refugee law currently affords no protections to those escaping life-threatening poverty since it limits the definition of "refugee" to those fleeing persecution.

In these circumstances, the "illegal" crossing of borders, which so preoccupies the newly-elected Donald Trump and right-wing populists across Europe, might actually be considered a justifiable form of resistance and civil disobedience against the economic injustice of the global order.

Is a Right to Move Plausible?

Many will be tempted to dismiss these arguments as the utopian fantasies of philosophers which fly in the face of basic common sense. Or they might point to the unacceptable level of cost and disruption which they predict will be the consequence of opening borders.

Yet we should reflect on the fact that many previous injustices, such as the institution of slavery, seemed like common sense at the time. The arguments given back then against abolition — based on its likely cost and disruption to slave-owning societies — seem perverse and wholly unconvincing today.

A more principled argument for restrictive border controls could be mounted on the basis of a state's right to self-determination or on the purported rights of a nation to preserve its cultural identity. Some philosophers, such as the British political theorist David Miller, have attempted arguments along these lines.

But I think these philosophical arguments against a right to move are ultimately unconvincing. They fail to give sufficient weight to the essential interest that all of us have in being able to live, love, study, work and settle without being restricted by the coercive and often violent imposition of borders. In the context of massive inequality, the current border regime is even more unjustified, akin to the arbitrary and anti-human character of a global caste system.

Those who believe in more open borders are currently on the political defensive in Britain and elsewhere. With much of the debate framed in narrow terms around migrant "skills" and "economic contributions," it is important not to lose sight of immigration as a moral issue.

If we approach it in this way, we will surely conclude that the current border regime is unjust and indefensible.

14

The Swiss Example

Vasco Pedrina

Vasco Pedrina is the former president of Unia, a Swiss trade union with 200,000 members. He also writes for the Guardian.

Switzerland presents another idea of what a world with open borders could look like, as just under 25 percent of the nation's population is foreign born. Looking at how Switzerland has navigated the past half-century illustrates how macro and micro economies react to an open and constant flow of people, labor, and goods. It also demonstrates how governments can mitigate many of the issues often associated with open borders.

A rguments about immigration have polarised between restriction and liberalisation. But key are accompanying measures to ensure freedom of movement is associated with wage and social protection.

Together with Luxembourg, Switzerland is one of the countries with the highest proportion of foreign nationals: they are responsible for one third of the country's total working hours. Due to Switzerland's higher wage-level, it finds itself more exposed to social and wage dumping than other countries.

It faces two major challenges in relation to the European Union. First, the EU is pressing Switzerland quickly to ratify a recently

"Curbs on migration or freedom of movement—the Swiss experience," by Vasco Pedrina, Social Europe. Reprinted by permission.

negotiated framework agreement, which aims to ensure close bilateral relations become closer.

But this framework agreement unacceptably calls into question existing wage-protection arrangements, or "flanking measures to the free movement of persons" (FlaM). A call to oppose it, in favour of "a social Europe, freedom of movement and strong workers' rights," has been signed by more than 2,000 personalities, including trade unionists, lawyers and academics.

Secondly, next year the Swiss people will vote in a referendum launched by the right-wing populist *Schweizerische Volkspartei*. The "SVP termination referendum" aims to achieve a "Swissexit." Its success would not only lead to the termination of the agreement on freedom of movement—as well as the abolition of wage-protection measures guaranteed by the FlaM—but would also mean the end of all bilateral agreements between Switzerland and the EU.

In this context the publication "Trade union migration policy in Switzerland and the fight against discrimination and social dumping" deals with our instructive history—in particular, with the comparison between the old quota system and the current system of freedom of movement accompanied by strong flanking measures.

Quota Policy

The economic boom after the second world war triggered high levels of immigration in Switzerland, particularly of seasonal workers. Until the 1960s, the government implemented a rotation policy which recognised migration as a purely transitory phenomenon.

Bowing to the pressure of a growing xenophobia, trade unions were the first to demand stricter quotas. The fact that trade unions helped to introduce the quota policy explains their difficulty in bringing about a "Copernican paradigm shift" towards an open immigration model.

In the past, the Swiss government tried to limit immigration in every way possible and to prevent migrants from becoming an integral part of society. But the rotation policy and the increasingly restrictive admission policy did not change the fact that the economy has always obtained the migrant labour-power it needed—legally or illegally.

The quota system was discriminatory. The quotas and the seasonal status of foreign nationals were always inseparable. Each tightening of the quota policy led to increased discrimination against migrant workers.

Despite its long-held seasonal-status policy, Switzerland has been unable to prevent migrants from settling with their families and becoming a valued part of society. Furthermore, the quota system failed to protect workers' employment and wages. On the contrary, the far lower wages of seasonal and cross-border workers and other migrants put all workers' wages under severe pressure—the same can be said regarding undeclared work. In addition, the system caused economic damage.

Free Movement

In this context, the shift in trade unions' migration policy, leading to their support for the introduction of the free movement of persons (FMP) with the EU in the 1990s, should not be underestimated. With the Bilateral Agreements between Switzerland and the EU of 2000, FMP has given everyone greater fundamental freedoms—in particular, more equal economic rights.

The flanking measures (FlaM) have meanwhile provided more effective instruments for wage and employment protection than any quota system. Furthermore, these changes have encouraged the immigration of skilled workers and thus supported more productive economic structures.

The FlaM bring together the two pillars of social protection and non-discriminatory policy. Free movement of persons with measures to protect workers' wages is also superior to uncontrolled FMP, where wage protection would be lacking.

Although the comparison between the two migration models produces a clear result, FMP remains in the crosshairs of certain political forces. Its future is far from guaranteed. A return to the dark days of the quota system is quite possible if one takes voters' growing concerns seriously—not to speak of the success of the nationalist right. Preventing the latter from imposing its aims will be one of the greatest challenges for trade unions and the left.

Human Rights

Developing a coherent and effective response to widespread cultural prejudice and resentment is a difficult task. But it is up to progressives to raise the banner of human rights, equal rights and active solidarity.

FMP has become the scapegoat for all problems in the labour market and society in general. The increasing internationalisation of the economy, the growing precariousness of labour relations and increasingly rapid changes with the digital revolution would, of course, also occur without it. Their negative social consequences— real, assumed or expected—are inherently linked to the way in which capitalism currently works.

FMP as an acquired right can only be maintained if we are able to place people's social problems at the centre of society's attention and make a substantial contribution to their resolution. This entails protection of jobs, wages and workers' rights. In the context of FMP, the fight to defend and develop the FlaM remains central.

Catastrophic Consequences

But this will not be enough. The gradual deterioration of the labour market shows, in the extreme case of the southern canton Ticino (on the border with Lombardy), that wage and social dumping has a strong cross-border component. It also shows that, without an effective antidote, criminal networks can continue to spread, with catastrophic consequences for the workers concerned—as well as for acceptance of an open Europe.

Cross-border wage dumping must be tackled with transnational measures, including via the new European Labour Authority, a European minimum-wage strategy and a "Marshall plan."

FMP is far more progressive than any quantitative immigration-limitation regime and guarantees workers the right to move freely. Maintaining it demands not only continued commitment to strong wage protection in Switzerland but also a Europe committed to such measures—and a convergence policy that can significantly reduce the vast wage disparities across the union.

15

How Open Borders Help Workers Around the World

Kevin Shih

Kevin Shih is an assistant professor in the department of economics at the City University of New York.

Conventional wisdom holds that open borders allow an unrestricted flow of immigrants into a country and that wages will go down as workers lose market power due to greater competition. Some studies, however, suggest otherwise. Kevin Shih writes about how the free flow of workers creates a labor market that is dynamic and reacts quickly and efficiently to population changes. In fact, according to this viewpoint, the local population expansion that immigration often entails has historically caused economies to grow rather than shrink.

Immigrants have long been a scapegoat when economies are sputtering, jobs are being lost or security is a concern.

President Donald Trump's planned wall along the Mexican border, for example, is premised on the notion that immigrants are pouring across the border (they're not), taking Americans' jobs (they haven't) and committing a disproportionate share of crimes (they don't).

The presumed threats of immigration were also front and center in Trump administration discussions on deporting millions of people who are in the U.S. illegally.

We saw something similar when U.K. voters opted for a "Brexit" from the European Union last year, when many British politicians cast immigrants as a threat to the physical, social and economic welfare of natives.

While it has become a popular notion in the West that immigrants jeopardize the job prospects of natives, over 30 years of economic research (including my own) give strong reason to believe otherwise.

And in fact, the opposite may be more likely: There's evidence immigrants actually promote economic growth.

Why We Blame Immigrants for Our Problems

Extensive reviews of research on the topic show that most studies of how immigration affects native wages and employment found very little effect.

Although economists have yet to arrive at a complete consensus, decades of studies generally do not support the notion that immigration harms the economy, market wages or native employment. So why do so many believe it when research suggests otherwise?

A central issue is that it is easy to think that the labor market is a zero-sum game and the number of jobs available is fixed. If everyone were competing over a finite number of jobs, more immigrants would mean fewer opportunities for natives, and vice versa, right? The reality, however, is much more complex, as I will show. Further, it is simply false to think of the number of jobs as fixed in the first place. Employment has been generally rising since 2010, which means more jobs for everyone.

A new migrant interested in the same job as you may diminish your odds a little, but a single immigrant with a good idea might end up creating hundreds or thousands of jobs that wouldn't have existed had he or she not crossed an ocean or border (the impact of son-of-a-migrant Steve Jobs or South African tech entrepreneur Elon Musk comes to mind).

The labor market is dynamic, and both individual workers and employers constantly readjust to changing conditions. In fact, many economists have found evidence that natives quickly adjust to the labor market forces of immigration and in a way that often yields positive benefits.

Adjusting to Immigration

Immigration flows into the U.S. do not affect all sectors equally. Immigrants are highly overrepresented in either very low-skilled manual and labor-intensive jobs or very high-skilled science and engineering occupations.

The types of immigrants who arrive and the areas in which they work are crucial for understanding the impact, and this concentration makes it possible to adjust to it.

In a 2010 study, Dartmouth economist Ethan Lewis found that companies in regions that saw inflows of less-skilled immigrants in recent decades adopted capital machinery at a lower rate.

Another study by Lewis and researchers Michael Clemens and Hannah Postel focused on an effort by the U.S. government in the 1960s to improve labor market conditions for native workers and boost their wages by excluding about a half-million seasonal workers from Mexico (braceros). It had precisely the opposite effect: Instead of raising wages or hiring more locals, farm owners reacted by adopting technologies that required less labor. The owners even switched their crops from ones that were less labor-intensive to ones whose production could be more easily mechanized.

In other words, the ability of businesses to substitute between technology and less-skilled immigrant workers means wages won't necessarily fall when immigration rises. And conversely, this means excluding or limiting immigration won't necessarily lift wages or benefit natives in other ways.

Economists Giovanni Peri and Chad Sparber found that inflows of immigrants—whether low- or high-skilled—induced native workers to shift to jobs that are more complementary in nature and where they have a comparative advantage. This type of shifting also limits the impact on native wages and employment.

For example, natives working in fields receiving large inflows of low-skilled immigrants—who had a comparative advantage in manual and physical labor—moved toward occupations requiring more communication-intensive tasks. They observed a similar phenomenon when high-skilled immigrants with comparative advantages in fields like science and mathematics enter the U.S. labor force. Rather than being laid off, native skilled workers moved to occupations that required more managerial and communication skills.

Just as natives move toward occupations in which they possess a comparative advantage relative to immigrants, they can also move across skill groups by acquiring education. Several economic papers, like ones by Jennifer Hunt and Will Olney and Dan Hickman, found that natives tend to acquire more education following the arrival of less-skilled immigrants. Increases in education benefit the long-term prospects of natives, and means they are no longer competing in the less-skilled labor market.

Growing the Economic Pie

But beyond simply doing no or little harm to natives, there's evidence immigrants actually benefit the overall economy—which helps everyone.

Recall that immigrants in the U.S. are highly represented in high-skill science and engineering occupations. Economists have long understood that economic growth is generated by innovation, which in turn comes from research and development. A study by Stanford economist Charles Jones found that nearly half of U.S. economic growth since the 1950s is attributable to the increase in the number of scientists and engineers engaged in research and development.

Combine this with the fact that about half of the growth in the number of scientists and engineers in the U.S. since the 1980s was due to immigrants and it is not difficult to understand the connection between skilled immigration and economic prosperity.

In a recent paper, coauthored with Giovanni Peri and Chad Sparber, I formally tested this idea. We examined whether increases in skilled foreign-born scientists and engineers in the U.S. from 1980 to 2010 improved productivity. We found modest gains in real wages for native skilled workers. And no negative impacts on native employment.

Complementing our finding is research by economists William Kerr and William Lincoln, who found that skilled immigrants increase innovation, thereby generating productivity gains for native workers most ready to take advantage of such technological advances.

As long as immigrants continue to innovate and invent, they can continue to boost economic growth.

Who Is Actually Most Hurt by Immigration?

Although most studies don't find adverse impacts on natives, that does not mean they have not found adverse impacts at all. In fact, the group that most commonly appears to be negatively affected by new immigrants are other recent immigrants.

Recent immigrants are the most easily substituted with new immigrants, tend to live and work in the same labor markets that new immigrants enter, often do not have the skills to move toward communication-intensive jobs and face restrictive policies that limit access to higher education. As such, their labor market prospects appear to deteriorate when new immigrants arrive.

Other studies that take a general focus on the labor market and find negative effects have been debated from time to time among academics, however, with little consensus.

A recent paper, however, calls into question many of these negative findings, showing researchers have been using measures of immigration that carry an inherent negative bias. Using correct measures eliminates the negative impact.

Facts Are Facts

All in all, most of the research suggests that the fear that immigration will drastically harm native wages and job prospects is by and large unsubstantiated. In fact, much work has shown the labor market is dynamic, and that native workers and employers take measures to evade any competitive forces from immigration.

While some pundits and presidential candidates will likely continue to claim immigration is harming our economy, that won't alter the evidence economists have uncovered in study after study. By the same token, claims that immigrants are flooding across our southern border (so we need a giant wall to keep them out) doesn't change the fact that illegal immigration to the U.S. has actually been falling for the past nine years.

Though it is easy to believe that foreigners will overcrowd a frail, zero-sum labor market, decades of research has shown the only thing that sums to zero are the estimated effects of immigration.

16

Why Open Borders Are Essential to the Global Economy

Mary Jo Dudley

Mary Jo Dudley is a faculty member in the department of development sociology at Cornell University and is the director of the Cornell Farmworker Program.

The millions of workers who enter the United States illegally are a vital part of the country's agricultural industry and its tax base; the annual free flow of seasonal workers across the American-Mexican border is what puts groceries on the shelves of supermarkets. Without this regular and massive influx, Mary Jo Dudley writes, fields would go unpicked and fruit would rot. Despite the political controversy surrounding illegal immigration, studies indicate that the majority of Americans believe these immigrants have a generally positive impact on the country.

The nation's attention is once again focused on the southern border, where President Trump claims the U.S. is facing a "crisis" over illegal immigration.

Immigrants play vital roles in the U.S. economy, erecting American buildings, picking American apples and grapes and taking care of American babies. Oh, and paying American taxes.

"Why care about undocumented immigrants? For one thing, they've become vital to key sectors of the US economy," by Mary Jo Dudley, The Conversation, January 15, 2019. https://theconversation.com/why-care-about-undocumented-immigrants-for-one-thing-theyve-become-vital-to-key-sectors-of-the-us-economy-98790. Licensed under CC BY-ND 4.0 International.

My work as the director of the Cornell Farmworker Program involves meeting with undocumented workers in New York, and the farmers who employ them. Here's a snapshot of who they are, where they work—and why Americans should care about them.

A Snapshot of Who They Are

Pew Research Center estimates that about 11.3 million people are currently living in the U.S. without authorization, down from a peak of 12.2 million in 2007. More than half come from Mexico, and about 15 percent come from other parts Latin America.

About 8 million of them have jobs, making up 5 percent of the U.S. workforce, figures that have remained more or less steady for the past decade.

Geographically, these unauthorized workers are spread throughout the U.S. but are unsurprisingly most concentrated in border states like California and Texas, where they make up about 9 percent of both states' workforces, while in Nevada, their share is over 10 percent.

Their representation in particular industries is even more pronounced, and the Department of Agriculture estimates that about half of the nation's farmworkers are unauthorized, while 15 percent of those in construction lack papers—more than the share of legal immigrants in either industry. In the service sector, which would include jobs such as fast food and domestic help, the figure is about 9 percent.

Further studies show that the importance of this population of workers will only grow in coming years. For example, in 2014, unauthorized immigrants made up 24 percent of maids and cleaners, an occupation expected to need 112,000 more workers by 2024. In construction, the number of additional laborers needed is estimated at close to 150,000. And while only 4 percent of personal care and home health aides are undocumented, the U.S. will soon require more than 800,000 people to fill the jobs necessary to take care of retiring baby boomers.

Vital to American Farms

Since agriculture is the industry that's most reliant on undocumented workers—and it's my area of expertise and research—let's zoom in on it.

Overall, the agricultural industry in the United States has been on the decline since 1950. Back then, farming was a family business that employed more than 10 million workers, 77 percent of whom were classified as "family." As of 2000—the latest such data available – only 3 million work on farms, and as noted earlier, an estimated half are undocumented.

Increasingly, dairy farms such as those in New York rely on workers from Mexico and Guatemala, many of whom are believed to be undocumented. Currently, there is no visa program for year-round workers on dairy farms, so the precarious status of these workers poses serious concerns for the economic viability of the dairy industry.

In 2017 research conducted by the Cornell Farmworker Program, 30 New York dairy farmers told us they turned to undocumented workers because they were unable to find and keep reliable U.S. citizens to do the jobs. That's in part because farm work can be physically demanding, dirty and socially denigrated work. More importantly, it is one the most dangerous occupations in the U.S.

A study commissioned by the dairy industry suggested that if federal labor and immigration policies reduced the number of foreign-born workers by 50 percent, more than 3,500 dairy farms would close, leading to a big drop in milk production and a spike in prices of about 30 percent. Total elimination of immigrant labor would increase milk prices by 90 percent.

The U.S. fruit, vegetable and meat industries are similarly at risk, and without the help of unauthorized workers, production would drop and consumers would likely see higher prices.

This has become of particular concern as immigration enforcement in agricultural communities intensifies.

Although the focus is usually on the southern border, what happens in the north matters as well, in part because the Border Patrol's 100-mile jurisdiction means immigrants living in most of New England can be pursued anywhere. As such, the surge in immigration enforcement along the border with Canada in recent years has resulted in more farmworkers being deported.

It also has meant fresh produce has been gone unpicked, left to rot in fields. One New York apple grower told us that due to labor shortages and dwindling prices for his red delicious variety, he plans to let his 100-year-old orchard go, because any investments in production would result in significant economic loss.

Who Cares? Most Americans

Judging by the pronouncements from the White House, you might think most people don't realize how integral undocumented immigrants are to the U.S. economy. But in fact, polls suggest that Americans do understand this, and also don't believe that immigrants take their jobs.

In a poll Cornell conducted in 2017, we asked New Yorkers, "How do you believe undocumented farmworkers impact local communities?"

About 75 percent of those we polled said they have "generally positive impacts," up from 62 percent in 2008. Of those who had a positive impression, most said it was because migrants fill jobs unwanted by citizens or provide essential farm help and keep prices low.

And national polling backs this up. A 2016 Pew poll found that 76 percent believe undocumented immigrants are as honest and hard-working as U.S. citizens, while 71 percent said they mostly fill jobs that Americans aren't willing to do.

Not only are there lots of reasons to care, the vast majority of Americans actually do.

17

Moral and Political Arguments for Open Borders

Aisha Dodwell

Aisha Dodwell is a political activist and campaigner for social justice. She is the Campaigns and Policy Officer at Global Justice Now.

According to Aisha Dodwell, open borders around the world would be beneficial for a wide range of reasons. They would reduce global inequality and violence while enabling countries to become richer and safer. According to Dodwell, borders are already largely nonexistent when it comes to the movement of money between countries, so why should individuals be subjected to greater restrictions? Furthermore, while opening borders would clearly mean that people could freely enter other countries, it would also mean that immigrants could safely return home to their families if desired.

B rexit has left three million EU citizens in Britain in a state of limbo, fearful that their lives could be torn apart by the end of free movement within the European Union.

But while the EU has stood firm on free movement within the single market, for those outside the union it has become "Fortress Europe." Europe's external borders have become the most violent in the world—more people die at Europe's borders than any other border worldwide.

"7 reasons why we should have open borders," by Aisha Dodwell, www.newint.org, November 29, 2017. Reprinted by kind permission of New Internationalist. © 2019 New Internationalist.

If we care about poverty and justice overseas, we need to start working towards a world of globally open borders for all.

Here's why:

Borders Are a Form of Global Apartheid

Borders preserve the privilege of the wealthy at the expense of the poor. They do this by preventing the movement of the world's poorest people, restricting their access to the resources and opportunities available in wealthy countries.

Modern immigration rules exist to enable those in power to keep out anyone deemed "unwanted." The first such law in Britain, the 1905 Aliens Act, gave Britain the power to 'prevent the landing of undesirable immigrants,' widely acknowledged to have been aimed at curbing Jewish immigration from Eastern Europe, the 'unwanted migrants' of that era.

Likewise, Britain's border regime today is focused on keeping out undesired people. Punitive immigration policies mean that families are routinely torn apart for not having enough money, and people are criminalized simply for seeking safety, or a better life.

Many of these people left their homes because of reasons outside their control, whether that was conflict, poverty, economic injustice or climate change. The UN's Refugee Agency estimates that 20 people are forced to flee their homes every second.

With global inequality at unprecedented levels, modern borders have become a form of global apartheid: segregating who can and can't access resources and opportunity.

Borders Produce Violence but Do Not Stop Immigration

The number of people dying while crossing borders has reached unprecedented levels.

Last year, over 5,000 people died in the Mediterranean attempting to reach Europe. Instead of offering safe passage, Europe has intensified its border enforcement and forced people to take more perilous journeys.

Projects such as the EU's Operation Sophia, a Naval mission patrolling the seas near Libya in order to stop, search and destroy smugglers' boats, has only made people's journeys more dangerous as it led to cheaper and more dangerous rubber dinghies being used.

And then there are Europe's violent outsourced borders in places such as Libya, where despite UN reports of widespread abuse and violence, Europe continues to fund migrant detention camps.

Even if people do reach Europe, they will likely be faced by further violence or incarceration under Europe's system of mass detention and deportation. In Britain alone, over 30,000 people are locked up in immigration detention centres each year. And the situation is the same in other wealthy pockets across the globe where the world's poor are routinely locked out. Australia notoriously sends people seeking asylum to outsourced detention camps in Papua New Guinea. While in the USA, which operates the largest immigration detention system, some 350,000 people passed through immigration detention last year.

The related policy of mass deportation means even those who make it to Europe are often sent back to the very violence and hardship they fled from in the first place. Europe's deadly deportation schemes such as the Joint Way Forward deal with Afghanistan means people are returned to countries where they risk persecution, torture and even death.

In Britain there is even an explicit policy aiming to create a "hostile environment" for migrants—launched by the current prime minister, Theresa May, when she was Home Secretary. Bank managers, NHS staff and landlords are routinely required to perform the role of immigration officers, monitoring people's immigration status, as borders increasingly become part of everyday life and the government forces undocumented migrants further underground.

But these deterrents and brutal border enforcement policies don't prevent people migrating. They simply make their journeys harder and often force them into the hands of smugglers.

Blaming Migrants for Low Wages Divides Workers and Creates a Race to the Bottom

Excluding migrants from work and refusing them access to basic services, as countries like Britain do, means they are often stopped from contributing to society and the economy.

Because they are then forced to work in the shadow economy, they also often end up working for below minimum wage, which pushes down labour standards. But where they are allowed to work legally, this is not the case.

Study after study shows how wages are only ever minimally affected, if at all, by immigration. Possibly the most detailed study on this issue comes from Denmark. Economists followed the wages and employment of every worker in the country between 1991 and 2008, and monitored the impacts of large influxes of refugees. They found that low-skilled wages and employment actually rose in response to the influx of refugees. Simply put, this is because immigrants are not just workers, but they also consume goods and take part in society, which in turn creates jobs.

Even if migrants did lower wages or reduce jobs, that should not be a reason to construct more brutal borders: who would argue now that women should be excluded from the workplace on the same grounds?

Instead of building borders, we should organize and fight for better rights for all working people, whatever their country of birth.

More Migrants Would Be Able to Return Home Safely

Open borders would mean that people could move freely, helping more immigrants return back home with the risks associated with crossing borders removed. For example, in the 1960s, 70 million Mexicans crossed into the USA, 85 per cent of whom returned later returned to Mexico. As the US border has become heavily militarized in recent decades, however, it has increased the dangerous associated with moving, and thus discouraged immigrants from going back.

Open Borders Would Make the World a Richer Place

According to economist Michael Clemens, opening the world's borders could double global GDP. That is because the change in a worker's location to a higher value economy increases their economic productivity. And because migrant workers often send money back to their country of origin through remittances, migration can have a positive impact on developing countries' economies too.

In addition, according to the Organization for Economic Co-operation and Development (OECD), across Europe, the average immigrant household contributes more in taxes than they take in benefits.

Of course, the economic value of a human being should never be the sole basis on which to allow them to exercise the right to move—and neither is GDP or economic growth the best measure of wellbeing. But we can be reassured that the world's economy would not collapse under a system of open borders.

We Can't Have Free Movement for Some and Not for All

Let's be honest, most people are already in favour of free movement—at least for themselves.

Europeans have always exercised this right, such as the hundreds of thousands who migrated to North America in the 17th and 18th centuries. Citizens of rich countries continue to do the same today. In fact, immigration control, in the modern sense of the term is a recent concept. Before the 1962 Commonwealth Immigration Act, people from Commonwealth countries like Kenya and India could come freely to Britain. It was only in reaction to xenophobic scaremongering by people like Enoch Powell that this changed.

We rarely hear opponents of free movement arguing to curtail their own rights to move, live, work, study or travel. Arguments for preventing free movement are always presented with the assumption that it is the movement of "others" being stopped.

The current system of border controls is such that the accident of birth determines the extent to which you can exercise the right to free movement. As a British passport holder you are entitled to travel to 173 countries without even a visa. If you're from Afghanistan, that number is 28.

Capital, Big Business and the Rich Already Have Open Borders—It's Time to Extend That to Everyone

We're told that global free movement is a pipe dream. But the truth is that it already exists—for the rich.

Borders barely exist for the movement of capital, and multinational companies can easily cross borders to extract resources and exploit labour.

Meanwhile, the world's richest people can buy citizenship of many countries, including within the EU. In Cyprus you can buy citizenship for a €2 million investment, while Portugal offers full residency and only asks for a mere €500,000 investment. The UK, too, offers a similar scheme in exchange for a £2 million investment.

The xenophobic media, which is so loud in its calls to stop desperate people fleeing the horrors of so-called Islamic State, is strangely quiet about the free movement of billionaires and oligarchs—and their rights to snap up luxury accommodation in cities like London, while pushing out the poor.

It is fundamentally unfair that corporate bosses can move jobs across the world, while ordinary workers do not have the freedom to move themselves. We should be controlling capital and freeing people, not the other way round.

We might not be able to open all borders tomorrow, but the first step is to begin working towards achieving the conditions that could make this a reality, for example through a universal minimum wage and global standards for workers' rights.

This might sound like a naive utopian dream today, but so too did many major struggles for social change in the past, until people fought for them—and won.

18

Socially Constructed Differences Create Borders and Refugee Crises

Jane Freedman

Jane Freedman is a professor of politics at University of Paris VIII in Saint-Denis, France. Her research focuses on issues related to gender, violence, conflict, and migration.

As of 2019, the number of displaced people in the world is higher than ever before, with a wide range of causes to blame for this. The responses by individual countries and the international community have not been sufficient to address the issue of displacement, and many refugees suffer as a result. This is partially because international laws fail to recognize and protect certain displaced groups as refugees, falling behind changing geopolitical realities. In other cases it is because countries feel they are shouldering too much of the burden of refugee crises. Efforts to "share responsibility" could also come with their own issues.

In 2019 UNHCR announced that the number of people displaced in the world had reached the highest number ever at 70.8 million[1]. Causes of displacement are multiple and complex—armed conflicts, persecution and discrimination (including gender-based forms of violence), structural violence and inequality. The conflict in Syria has by itself led to the forced displacement of

"Grand Challenges: Refugees and Conflict," by Jane Freedman, Frontiers in Human Dynamics, October 30, 2019, https://www.frontiersin.org/articles/10.3389/fhumd.2019.00001/full. Licensed under CC BY 4.0 International.

over ten million people, of whom over four million have crossed borders into neighboring countries. And whilst the number of people forced to move from their homes increases, the responses to displacement both national and international are still not sufficient to offer protection and security to refugees. Many of the world's wealthier countries are in the process of building walls and reinforcing border security to attempt to prevent refugees from reaching their territory. However, the vast majority of refugees remain in poorer countries, either in massive refugee camps, or struggling to survive in urban centers and their peripheries.

Recent research has advanced our understanding of the causes of forced displacement and the experiences of refugees, and in doing so has questioned the utility of the categorizations imposed by international law and politics, which for example, divide refugees from economic migrants, and distinguish between forced and voluntary migration. This questioning of categories opens up interesting definitional questions: who is a refugee? Are existing international laws and conventions sufficient to offer protection? Or do they need to be adapted to changing geopolitical realities? The impacts of climate change on migration, for example, has led to a debate over whether a new group of "climate refugees" should be recognized under international law? These debates on categorization and definitions add to existing critiques of international refugee conventions and policies, which have pointed to the ways in which these exclude groups such as victims of gender-based forms of persecution.

Widespread images of people trying to cross newly built walls and fences at international borders, or being rescued from sinking ships as they attempt to cross sea borders, have brought into stark relief the impacts of the increasing securitization of migration across the world. Securitization of migration and closing of borders has led to increasing violence and insecurities for refugees themselves, without having any real impact on decreasing migration flows. Refugees are being forced into taking increasingly expensive and dangerous routes to reach their countries of destination, and many are dying on the route. And these experiences of violence and insecurity vary according to the social, economic and political structures of inequality in countries of origin, transit and destination. We need to understand more the ways in which securitization has a direct impact on the experiences of individuals and the ways that gendered and racialized forms of insecurity are manifested during refugee journeys. For those refugees who survive these dangerous journeys, conditions of reception in countries of destination are also often inadequate. Recent reports have highlighted the insalubrious and dangerous conditions for refugees living in hotspots on the Greek islands for example. Many refugees now find themselves trapped in dirty and overcrowded camps as a result of the EU-Turkey agreement of March 2016 and of the reluctance of other EU Member States to relocate some of these refugees and settle them in their own countries.

And whilst much attention has focused on the so-called refugee "crises" in Europe and other rich countries, we must remember that the majority of the world's refugees still live in the global South, frequently in countries bordering their own. Too little attention is being paid to the ways in which these poorer countries are impacted by hosting refugees, and what the refugees' experiences are within these countries, whether in camps or as urban refugees.

The Global Compact on Refugees[2] a new international agreement on refugees signed in 2018 was announced by the international community as a way forward for "sharing responsibility" for refugee protection and has been hailed by some as a welcome advance. However, critics have pointed to the fact that the Compact, despite its promise to pay more attention to the "root causes" of refugee flows, and to encourage all States to share responsibility for protection, might actually prove a step backwards as it may dilute the international principles of refugee law, and weaken protection of women and children. Further research is necessary to understand what if any impact this new Compact might have, and whether richer States will in fact agree to share greater responsibility for protection of refugees with the nations which currently host large refugee populations. The fact that the Compact is a non-binding agreement, with no concrete measures for responsibility sharing seems to indicate that current policies of securitization of borders and refoulement of refugees by the US, European Union Member States and other richer countries will continue.

Restrictive policies on refugee movement have fuelled and been fuelled by various public and media representations of these refugees as some kind of "threat" to host countries and/or "undeserving" of support. These media representations and the impacts that they have both on public opinion and on policymaking on refugees is a subject that merits further research and analysis. The ubiquity of discourses representing refugees as a threat might indicate that public opinion is in favor of more restrictive policies to prevent refugees from arriving in host countries. But this perception should be nuanced with a consideration of the various solidarity movements with refugees which have developed and strengthened, including initiatives to rescue refugees from the Mediterranean, to provide accommodation and food, or other forms of solidarity and protest against exclusionary politics. Solidarity can help to support inclusion and integration of refugees into host societies and these solidarity movements might also be seen to help refugees to exercise their agency and to recreate new forms of citizenship.

It is vital that research on issues related to refugees not consider these refugees merely as "victims" of violence and conflict and displacement but takes into account their agency as actors. How do refugees themselves see their situation, and how do they plan their strategies both for flight and for integration into new societies? These are among the many questions and pressing challenges with which research should be concerned. And across all of these questions and issues, researchers should take an approach which highlights differences of gender, sexual orientation, class, ethnicity, race, nationality, age, ability, and so on, to ensure that neither refugees, nor host communities are considered as homogeneous and monolithic, and that the impacts of all of these socially constructed differences on the experience of displacement and migration are fully considered. It is clear that numbers of refugees will not diminish significantly in the near future, so we must be concerned with answering these questions and to provide recommendations and solutions that will ensure better protection for those impacted by displacement, and reduce the insecurities and violence faced by refugees across the world.

Notes

1. https://www.unhcr.org/figures-at-a-glance.html
2. Global Compact on Refugees, UN doc A/73/12 (Part II) (2 August 2018); Global Compact for Safe, Orderly and Regular Migration, UN doc A/RES/73/195 (19 December 2018).

19

The Schengen Area: Free Movement Is Good for Business

Aleksej Heinze

Aleksej Heinze is a senior lecturer in the Centre for Digital Business at the University of Salford, United Kingdom, of which he is also the codirector.

The Schengen area in Europe was established in 1995 to allow the free movement of people between member countries. These include twenty-six European states across the continent, most of which are part of the European Union. These virtually open borders have allowed goods and services to travel quickly from country to country, which has significantly benefited businesses in the region. Attempts to add restrictions at borders would be detrimental to the economy and, furthermore, would not make sense in a marketplace that is largely digital and consequently already free from border restrictions.

The Schengen area has never been tested to the same level as it is now. The unprecedented volume of refugees and migrants arriving in Europe has left its leaders struggling to cope. Germany's chancellor, Angela Merkel, issued a sober warning that the crisis puts Schengen into question, while Italy says it is

"Business will suffer if border crossings between European neighbours are shut," by Aleksej Heinze, The Conversation, September 4, 2015, https://theconversation.com/business-will-suffer-if-border-crossings-between-european-neighbours-are-shut-47022. Licensed under CC BY-ND 4.0 International

ready to impose border controls and Hungary has sealed off its main train station.

The Schengen Agreement is one of Europe's most remarkable achievements. Implemented in 1995, it allows free movement of people between member countries—effectively removing border controls. It means that visas, rights of asylum and checks at borders outside the Schengen area apply across member states. Now, some are keen to argue, it is under threat.

The principle of Schengen is to bring countries closer together and increase international cooperation, trade and ultimately to aim for a peaceful resolution to disputes. One of the key benefits to businesses in the catchment area is the speed with which goods and services can travel across country borders — thus making them more competitive compared to those arriving from non-Schengen member states. It is a major factor contributing to the EU as the world's largest economic area.

The often hours-long delays that are normally a routine part of border crossing checks are a waste of time for companies wanting to transport goods or personnel to their destinations as soon as possible. Time is money after all.

To ensure the most efficient delivery of materials or services from suppliers to customers, organisations use Value Stream Mapping exercises. This is a management method where an organisation's every activity is evaluated in terms of how it adds value to the business. Businesses in Schengen member states have so far placed more value on the speed of transport facilitated by the freedom of movement than they have on the control of borders.

Digital Borders

Businesses today, in particular those involved in the digital economy, tend to ignore conventional country borders. The idea of free exchange—whether it be for employees to share information or crowdsource ideas—is a fundamental part of engaging with prospective customers.

Further, the idea of barriers being put up along physical borders runs in direct contrast to the technological revolution we've seen in recent years that has made the world feel much smaller and more interconnected. Social networks have become a normal part of life, allowing individuals to communicate across borders without having to even think about where the individuals you are talking to might be based.

This can be seen vividly when big international events take place such as the World Cup final last year.

At the European level, there has been a conscious drive for closer digital collaboration among EU member states—to form a Digital Single Market. The idea is to capitalise on the free movement principle and expand its reach to common trade standards for online purchases of goods and services.

These standards and agreements for the movement of parcels and services are based on Schengen's free movement principle being maintained. The approximate cost for the express parcels industry alone could be more than €80m a year. These costs would inevitably be passed on to consumers if changes are made to the Schengen Agreement.

Plus, if border controls were re-introduced, the impact on shipping times and costs would inevitably go up and will have to be paid by everyone who might travel or send goods or services within the EU. It would also be less enticing for online businesses to set themselves up in the European Economic Area.

Two thirds of business in the EU is conducted with other member states so change will affect most people. Most supermarkets, for example, rely on goods imported from other member states so food shoppers would all experience an increased financial burden.

The fact that countries that are not part of Schengen (such as the UK) are already feeling the pressure of an increase in migration shows that border controls and curbs to the agreement are unlikely to change matters.

Ultimately, the huge rise in refugees and migrants is a product of failed foreign policies and problems outside of Europe. Until these are resolved, Europe shouldn't shoot itself in the foot by implementing Schengen restrictions that are also likely to have a negative impact on the European economy.

20

Humanity Is Interconnected and Shares an Obligation

Karen Bravo

Karen Bravo is a professor of law at the Robert H. McKinney School of Law in Indiana, where she is also associate dean of graduate studies and international affairs.

All too often, the discourse surrounding immigration displays the tendency to dehumanize and "other" immigrants and refugees, treating them as a problem and a burden for a country to take on. Mobility with the intention of escaping threats and hardship has long characterized human behavior, but borders now stand in the way of this and create new obstacles for those in peril. Though governments use the rhetoric of providing a safe haven to refugees and of having a sense of obligation to the international community, their policies are often intended to deter newcomers. According to Bravo, border control and human rights are fundamentally at odds.

According to the latest figures from the International Office of Migration, over 700,000 migrants have arrived by sea into Europe in 2015.

But today's refugee crisis is not just about the movement of people. It is also about the human immobility that is embedded into the legal, political and economic systems of nation states across the world. That human immobility is now coming under extreme pressure.

Just how this institutional immobility is affecting migrants and their would-be host countries is the subject that I, as a scholar of human trafficking, want to explore in this article.

But, first, poetry—inspired by the children's verse Brown Bear, Brown Bear—to crystallize thought and shift perspectives.

What Do We See?

People, people, what do we see
We see a toddler's body washed by the sea
We see barbed wire stopping those that flee
We see bodies, dirty clothes, desperation and fear
We see the old and the young, crying, fleeing, dying
People, people, what do we see?
We see invasion, humanity, opportunism, chaos
We see profit, indifference, hatred, fear, welcome
We see meals, and diapers, and smugglers, and wi-fi
We see inhumanity, traffickers, the future, the past
Death giving and life dealing, and money-making too
People, people, what do we see?
We see divisions, breakings apart, failure and pain
We see compassion, and hate, and confusion, and welcome
We see humanity looking at us

Dueling Perceptions

Images of desperate humanity in inexorable motion flow across the world's televisions, newspapers and news feeds.

The movement from Syria is not singular: Africans, crowded into unseaworthy boats, have been coming from northern Africa toward Europe for years.

In 2014, in the United States, state and federal governments, as well as the public, panicked as the number of women-headed family groups and unaccompanied children crossing the US/ Mexico border increased.

Afghans, Iraqis, Rohingya (Muslims from Myanmar) and others are detained or turned back as they attempt sea crossings from Asia to Australia.

Mass human movements give rise to inherently conflicting reactions: instincts of compassion and welcome for desperate fellow human beings clash with impulses of exclusion and the desire to protect individual economies, cultures, and nations from outsiders.

Nation-states and their inhabitants struggle, then, with a dual perception: are these migrants to be seen as human beings fleeing danger and seeking haven from natural or manmade disasters? Or are they "others" who seek access to and a share of the resources accumulated and guarded within national borders?

Refugees Under International Law

According to the UN Refugee Convention, the majority of the world's states have agreed to give asylum to people who are deemed to be "refugees."

Most, if not all, of the European Union member states are signatories and accessories to this convention.

Indeed, it was Europe's refugee crises after World Wars I and II that inspired the convention. However, the provisions of the UN Refugee Convention appear to be inadequate to guide state behavior in the present crisis. The term "refugee" is narrowly defined, and as a result, some individuals seeking asylum are kept out. Different countries define refugee status—and the consequences of refusing to grant it—differently.

Political considerations—notably disagreements about how responsibility for the refugees should be allocated among European Union member states—also are obstacles to providing haven to individuals.

In fact, the sheer logistical challenge of the mass transfer of population appears to have overwhelmed the European system and psyche.

Kant's cosmopolitan right concerns relations between persons and foreign states.

As Benhabib writes:

hospitality is a "right" which belongs to all human beings insofar as we view them as potential participants in a world republic.

Furthermore, she argues, this right,

cannot be refused, if such refusal would involve the destruction—Kant's word here is Untergang—of the other. However, [Kant] distinguishes between a temporary sojourn—to which the stranger has a right, if s/he is peaceful— and a permanent stay, which would be enabled through different arrangements than those of the temporary sojourner.

The basis of the right of hospitality and consequent right to sojourn) was "common possession (or habitation) of the surface of the earth."

Benhabib's analysis of the contradiction between state sovereignty and border control on the one hand and human rights on the other leads her to the conclusion that the solution is what she calls "democratic iterations."

These, Benhabib explains, are

complex processes of public argument, deliberation, and learning through which universalist rights claims are contested and contextualized, invoked and revoked, throughout legal and political institutions as well as in the public sphere of liberal democracies.

In other words, through an ongoing process of formal and informal interactions within and between individual communities and governments, universal and enforceable concepts of common humanity will emerge.

To more effectively and humanely respond to today's "crisis," we need to understand and implement in political discourse— as we have in economic discourse—the interconnectedness and oneness of humanity.

Organizations to Contact

The editors have compiled the following list of organizations concerned with the issues debated in this book. The descriptions are derived from materials provided by the organizations. All have publications or information available for interested readers. The list was compiled on the date of publication of the present volume; the information provided here may change. Be aware that many organizations take several weeks or longer to respond to inquiries, so allow as much time as possible.

Free Migration Project
150 Cecil B. Moore Avenue, Suite 203
Philadelphia, PA 19122
email: david.bennion@freemigrate.org
website: www.freemigrationproject.org

The Free Migration Project is a Philadelphia-based nonprofit that advocates for the right of people to freely migrate. The group provides legal support to refugees and advocates for what the group calls fair and open immigration laws and the abolition of deportation.

FWD
1776 Massachusetts Avenue NW
Washington, DC 20036
email: info@fwd.us
website: www.fwd.us

A lobbying group that was created with the support of Facebook cofounder and CEO Mark Zuckerberg, FWD approaches the issue of immigration reform from the perspective of companies frustrated by the inability to bring skilled labor from countries around the world to the United States. In this way, FWD represents the demand for open borders coming from new tech companies that see the entire world as both their customer and their labor pools.

Migration Policy Institute
400 16th Street NW, Suite 300
Washington, DC 20036
phone: (202) 266-1940
email: mmittelstadt@migrationpolicy.org
website: www.migrationpolicy.org

The Migration Policy Institute is a DC-based think tank that was founded, in part, with money provided by the Ford Foundation, the J. M. Kaplan Fund, and Carnegie Corporation. It publishes an online journal called the *Migration Information Source*, a publication that covers issues in global migration. The publication creates an accessible source of information on the subject of migration.

Open Borders: The Case
email: openborders@googlegroups.com
website: www.openborders.info

A self-identified 'blog-cum-informational resource' with a stated goal of fostering a discussion of open borders from both sides of the issue, this libertarian-friendly publication was founded by Vipul Naik, a University of Chicago-educated data scientist who codes professionally.

Pueblo Sin Fronteras
2242 S. Damen Ave.
Chicago, IL 60608
phone: (760) 332-8631
email: refugeecaravan@gmail.com
website: www.pueblosinfronteras.org

With a name that translates to "Village Without Borders," the Chicago-based group came to prominence in 2018 when groups of refugees from a number of Central America countries—the so-called "caravans"—were assisted by activists affiliated with the group, which drew media attention in the United States.

Transactional Records Access Clearinghouse (TRAC)
Suite 360, Newhouse II
215 University Place
Syracuse, NY 13244-2100
phone: (315) 443-3563
email: trac@syr.edu
website: www.trac.syr.edu

The Transactional Records Access Clearinghouse is a tremendous resource for hard numbers on immigration detention in the United States. In recent years, immigration detentions have become a part of life for thousands of border crossers deemed questionable by the federal government. The information that TRAC provides gives numerical reality to a world too often conducted in the shadows.

United Nations High Commissioner for Refugees (UNHCR)
Case Postale 2500 CH-1211
Genève 2 Dépôt
Switzerland
phone: +41 22 739 8111
email: USAWA@unhcr.org
website: www.unhcr.org

The UNHCR is the UN agency responsible for assisting refugees. It was established in 1950 and is responsible for assisting with the transportation and settlement of refugees from around the world.

VERA Centre for Russian and Border Studies
Karelian Institute
University of Eastern Finland
Joensuu Campus
PO Box 111
FI-80101 Joensuu
Finland
phone: +358 (0) 294 45 1111
email: Jeremy.Smith@uef.fi
website: www.uef.fi/en/web/vera

The VERA Centre for Russian and Border Studies at the Karelian Institute of the University of Eastern Finland is a center for research on the subject of cross-border cooperation and migration between the countries of Finland and Russia, a contentious issue that flared into a military conflict in 1940. The institute's name comes from the Finnish words "venäjä" and "raja," which translate to "Russia" and "border," respectively.

Zolberg Institute on Migration and Mobility
79 Fifth Avenue, 16th Floor
New York, NY 10003
phone: (212) 229-5150
email: migration@newschool.edu.
website: www.zolberginstitute.org

The Zolberg Institute is part of the New School and was founded by Ary Zolberg in the 1990s. Since then, the Institute has been producing research on the political, economic, and cultural consequences of migration and aims to empower students to work with nonprofits to help facilitate the free movement of people around the world.

Bibliography

Books

Maurizio Ambrosini, Manlio Cinalli, and David Jacobson. *Migration, Borders and Citizenship: Between Policy and Public Spheres*. London, UK: Palgrave Macmillan, 2020.

Wendy Brown. *Walled States, Waning Sovereignty*. Brooklyn, NY: Zone Books, 2010.

Francisco Cantú. *The Line Becomes a River: Dispatches from the Border*. New York, NY: Penguin Random House, 2018.

Bryan Caplan. *Open Borders: The Science and Ethics of Immigration*. New York, NY: St. Martin's Press, 2019.

Justin Akers Chacón and Mike Davis. *No One Is Illegal: Fighting Racism and State Violence on the U.S.-Mexico Border*. Chicago, IL: Haymarket Books, 2006.

Porter Fox. *Northland: A 4,000-Mile Journey Along America's Forgotten Border*. New York, NY: W. W. Norton Company, 2019.

Greg Grandin, *The End of the Myth: From the Frontier to the Border Wall in the Mind of America*. New York, NY: Metropolitan Books, 2019.

Reece Jones. *Violent Borders*. Brooklyn, New York: Verso, 2017.

Reece Jones and Azmeary Ferdoush. *Borders and Mobility in South Asia and Beyond*. Amsterdam, NL: Amsterdam University Press, 2018.

Tim Marshall. *Divided: Why We're Living in an Age of Walls*. New York, NY: Simon & Schuster, 2019.

Sandro Mezzadra and Brett Neilson. *Border as Method, Or, the Multiplication of Labor*. Durham, NC: Duke University Press, 2013.

Todd Miller. *Empire of Borders*. Brooklyn, New York: Verso, 2019.

Grigoris Panoutsopoulos, Thanasis Lagios, and Vasia Lekka. *Borders, Bodies and Narratives of Crisis in Europe*. London, UK: Palgrave Macmillan, 2018.

Margaret Regan. *The Death of Josseline: Immigration Stories from the Arizona Borderlands*. New York, NY: Penguin Random House, 2010.

Eileen Truax. *We Built the Wall*. Brooklyn, New York: Verso, 2018.

Harsha Walia. *Undoing Border Imperialism*. Chico, CA: AK Press, 2013.

Keren Weitzberg. *We Do Not Have Borders: Greater Somalia and the Predicaments of Belonging in Kenya*. Athens, OH: Ohio University Press, 2017.

Periodicals and Internet Sources

Atossa Araxia Abrahamian, "There Is No Left Case for Nationalism," *Nation*, November 28, 2018, www.thenation.com/article/open-borders-nationalism-angela-nagle/.

Bernard Avishai, "The Meaning of Open Trade and Open Borders," *New Yorker*, October 17, 2017, www.newyorker.com/business/currency/the-meaning-of-open-trade-and-open-borders.

Benjamin Bossi, "Open Borders Is Just Another Form Of Foreign Intervention Doomed To Fail," *Federalist*, March 12, 2019, www.thefederalist.com/2019/03/12/open-borders-just-another-form-foreign-intervention-doomed-fail/.

Michael Clemens, "A world without borders makes economic sense," *Guardian*, September 4, 2011, www.theguardian.com/global-development/poverty-matters/2011/sep/05/migration-increase-global-economy.

"Europeans remain welcoming to immigrants," *Economist*, April 19, 2019, www.economist.com/graphic-detail/2018/04/19/europeans-remain-welcoming-to-immigrants.

Aaron Freedman, "Open Borders Made America Great," *New Republic*, August 9, 2019, www.newrepublic.com/article/154717/open-borders-made-america-great.

Adi Gaskell, "Making The Case For Open Borders," *Forbes*, May 17, 2019, www.forbes.com/sites/adigaskell/2019/05/17/making-the-case-for-open-borders/#615a6fb4577e.

Carlo Invernizzi-Accetti, "Why the left should argue for more immigration – but not open borders," *Guardian*, September 9, 2019, www.theguardian.com/commentisfree/2019/sep/09/left-immigration-open-borders.

Joshua Jelly-Schapiro, "What Are Borders For?," *New Yorker*, November 27, 2019, www.newyorker.com/books/under-review/what-are-borders-for.

Farhad Manjoo, "There's Nothing Wrong With Open Borders," *New York Times*, January 19, 2019, www.nytimes.com/2019/01/16/opinion/open-borders-immigration.html.

Angela Nagle, "The Left Case Against Open Borders," *American Affairs*, Winter 2018, www.americanaffairsjournal.org/2018/11/the-left-case-against-open-borders.

"The progressive case for immigration," *Economist*, May 18, 2017, www.economist.com/finance-and-economics/2017/03/18/the-progressive-case-for-immigration.

Shaun Raviv, "If People Could Immigrate Anywhere, Would Poverty Be Eliminated?" *Atlantic*, April 13, 2013, www.theatlantic.com/international/archive/2013/04/if-people-could-immigrate-anywhere-would-poverty-be-eliminated/275332.

Robin Simcox, "Open Borders Mean Closed Opportunities for National Prosperity," Heritage Foundation, July 8, 2019, www.heritage.org/immigration/commentary/open-borders-mean-closed-opportunities-national-prosperity.

Alex Tabarrok, "The Case for Getting Rid of Borders—Completely," *Atlantic*, October 10, 2015, www.theatlantic.com/business/archive/2015/10/get-rid-borders-completely/409501.

William T. Vollmann, "Just Keep Going North," *Harpers*, July 2019, harpers.org/archive/2019/07/just-keep-going-north/.

John Washington, "What Would an Open-Borders World Actually Look Like?" *Nation*, April 24, 2019, www.thenation.com/article/open-borders-immigration-asylum-refugees.

Index